China, Japan
and the European Community

China, Japan and the European Community

Robert Taylor

The Athlone Press
London
•
Fairleigh Dickinson University Press
Rutherford • Madison •Teaneck

First published 1990 by The Athlone Press Ltd
1 Park Drive, London NW11 7SG

© Robert Taylor 1990

British Library Cataloguing in Publication Data

Taylor, Robert, *1941-*
    China, Japan and the European Community.
    I. Title   330.951

    ISBN 0-485-11356-2

Library of Congress Cataloging-in-Publication Data

Taylor, Robert, 1941–
    China, Japan, and the European Community / Robert Taylor.
        p.   cm.
    Includes bibliographical references (p.   ) and index.
    ISBN 0-8386-3428-1
    (alk. paper)
    1. European Economic Community countries—Foreign economic
relations—China.   2. China—Foreign economic relations—European
Economic Community countries.   3. European Economic Community
countries—Foreign economic relations—Japan.   4. Japan—Foreign
economic relations—European Economic Community countries.
I. Title.
HF1532.935.C5T39   1990
337.5104—dc20   90-55154
                                                                                    CIP

Associated University Presses
440 Forsgate Drive
Cranbury, NJ 08512

The paper used in this publication meets the requirements of the American
National Standard for Permanence of Paper for Printed Library Materials
Z39.48-1984.

This edition is published by arrangement with
The Athlone Press, London.

PRINTED IN THE UNITED STATES OF AMERICA

Contents

Preface

Great power status used very often to derive from territorial conquest but now military strength, however crucial, is only one component of national power. In the 1980s the two superpowers have been shown as economically vulnerable: in the Soviet Union relative technological backwardness and inefficiency have prompt ed 'glasnost': United States pre-eminence has been eroded by massive trade deficits. In the race to acquire the innovative skills needed to compete in the twenty-first century the Japanese are well advanced, and if the promise of a unified market, scheduled for 1992, is fulfilled, the EC will become an even greater economic force. China, still technologically backward, has enlisted EC countries, among others, to aid her ambitious modernisation programme; an increasingly educated Chinese population and as yet virtually untapped abundant natural resources make her an emerging superpower. China remains a Communist country but at the present time her leaders appear to be placing a greater premium on economic growth at home than world revolution abroad.

As China, Japan and the EC define their new roles in international affairs, this book contrasts China–EC relations and Japan–EC relations.

Ever since European colonial powers opened China to trade in the mid-nineteenth century, Western merchants and industrialists have seen that land as a vast market eldorado of untold wealth waiting to be exploited. But, in the 1980s, as before, the reality is different; while vast natural resources mean great potential for China and her trading partners, progress is inhibited by a poor infrastructure, a paucity of energy supplies and industrial management practices unsuited to the rigours of international competition. It is, though, in helping to remedy such deficiencies that future EC–China economic co-operation undoubtedly lies.

In contrast, Japan, with fewer natural resources than China, successfully competed with Western powers on their own terms from the outset, and in spite of devastating defeat in the Pacific War has, in the short space of a hundred and fifty years, become the world's greatest creditor nation.

But Japan's post-war economic success has been at the expense of the living standards of ordinary Japanese; personal purchasing power, quality of housing and public amenities fall well below general levels in the EC. National wealth is still not reflected in the quality of life of Japanese citizens but the young upwardly mobile are demanding better services. Thus, with the high yen, opportunities abound for EC exporters who are only just beginning to penetrate the enormous Japanese market. Brand names of Japanese consumer goods have long since been household words in European countries; their EC counterparts may well achieve similar recognition in Japan, as the Japanese are compelled to stimulate domestic demand and open up their own consumer markets to foreign goods.

Coming from a small overcrowded archipelago, the Japanese must look with envy at the open spaces of the United States and even of Western Europe; on the other side individual EC countries are competing for Japanese investment and technological know-how. In technology, of course, EC countries also have their individual strengths, and such knowledge knows no national boundaries in a world of economic interdependence.

Moreover, as modern communications proliferate, and personal travel, technological co-operation and cultural exchanges increase, the societies of China and Japan will become more familiar and less exotic to the peoples of the EC. To date, however, Japanese market reconnaissance and study of the EC have been infinitely superior to equivalent European efforts vis-a-vis Japan; but Westerners will neglect to learn about Japanese language and culture at their own peril.

Over past centuries the centre of civilisation, if defined as including economic strength and technological innovation as well as military power, has shifted firstly from the Mediterranean and Graeco-Roman world to Western Europe and then to the Atlantic during the recent decades of American supremacy. The convergence of population drift to America's West Coast, the development of the Soviet Far East, the growing ascendancy of Japan and China's modernisation suggest that the twenty-first could be the Pacific century. Trends affecting two of the Asia-Pacific region's major powers, China and Japan, will inevitably have a bearing on the future of the EC.

Such far-reaching themes are the major foci of this book, and to take account of momentous developments during the last twelve months a postscript has been added.

Acknowledgements

This book has been written over a period of several years, during which time I have benefited from being able to discuss the major issues involved with fellow scholars as well as those concerned with the more practical aspects of East-West relations in EC countries.

I am especially indebted to Dr Werner Draguhn of the Institut fuer Asienkunde, Hamburg and Professor Joachim Glaubitz of the Institut fuer Wissenschaft und Politik, Munich, who put the excellent source materials and facilities available at their respective institutions at my disposal.

In addition, I would like to acknowledge a debt to the traders, industrialists and bankers who willingly gave me the benefit of their experience, particularly as it related to trade with China and Japan. The views expressed and the conclusions drawn in the text are, however, mine.

I am grateful for the provision of a grant from the German Academic Exchange Service which greatly facilitated my research in the Federal Republic of Germany in 1982.

Finally, I wish to thank Marjorie Gould, Beryl Stout and Janet Marks for typing various sections of the manuscript.

China, Japan
and the European Community

1
Introduction: Chinese and Japanese Views of the World

European perceptions of contemporary China and Japan are still largely conditioned by the differing responses of the two countries to the Western colonial impact of the mid-nineteenth century. The advanced industrial power required of Japan for World War II–laid the foundations for her phenomenal post-war economic growth but China remained economically underdeveloped, being perceived by the West as part of the Third World; only since the late 1970s, with the dedication of Chairman Mao Zedong's successors to an ambitious modernisation programme designed to quadruple agricultural and industrial production by the turn of the century, has China been seen as an emerging superpower.

In their relationships with the Western world, however, China and Japan have much more in common than at first sight; in spite of Japan's massive export thrust and China's growing role in international trade, both countries are to a large extent closed societies, often apparently beyond any proper understanding on the part of foreigners. Despite her present outward image of Western-style modernity and material prosperity, Japan's institutional behaviour is still marked by traditional—and uniquely Japanese—social values of authoritarian hierarchy and group loyalties, and these have so far precluded the European penetration of Japanese distribution systems for consumer goods to anything like the extent that the Japanese themselves have done in EC markets. In China's case the Communist Party came to power by mobilising the peasantry and exploiting the nationalist cause, promising to rid China of foreign domination, and then enshrined Marxism-Leninism (adapted to Chinese conditions) as the state's ideology, installing a command economy where the central government controls the allocation and distribution of resources on the Soviet model. But like Japan, China has a

Confucian heritage where personal relationships—through family, friends, or shared educational experiences, even in the context of Communist Party and state organisations—loom larger than the contractual Western-style legal obligations. Traditional patterns of political and social control have thus also informed the norms and values of Chinese communism.

If the Chinese and Japanese, through their own enlightened self-interest, seek economic co-operation, mutual investment and technological exchange with the West, especially the countries of the EC, a theme common to the foreign policies of both is that of independence from the two superpowers. By the Treaty of Friendship of 1950 China was allied to the Soviet Union but by 1960 the two countries were in open dispute; disagreements over how to promote world revolution and achieve their final goal of communism led to rivalry between national interests—the Chinese accusing the Russians of trying to exploit China economically and subverting the Chinese Communist Party (CCP) in the 1950s, and aiming to turn the country into a Soviet satellite. By the 1970s the Chinese leaders saw the Soviet Union as the more dangerous of the two superpowers, and for national security as well as economic reasons turned to forging links with Western countries including the USA and the EC. In the absence of strategic imports from the Soviet Union, China needed Western technology to sustain and promote its economic development.

To its adherents ideology is the repository of historical truth, and thus the CCP sought to explain and justify its policy towards the Western world. During the 1970s, Mao Zedong took account of the shifts in the international situation towards a multipolar world—that is to say, where there are differing views on confrontation and detente in both the Communist and Western blocs—by proclaiming the 'theory of the three worlds'. In the first world were the two superpowers, the USA and the Soviet Union; in the second, other industrialised countries especially those of Western Europe, Canada and Japan; and in the third, the developing countries of Asia, Africa and Latin America. In terms of both national security and economic interest the Chinese leaders were to use the Second World as a counterweight to their perceived enemy, the other superpower, the Soviet Union. Yet by the mid-1980s a greater flexibility appeared in the conduct of China's foreign policy, and the old rigid categories of friends and enemies gave way to a more balanced appraisal of how the constellation of world forces actually affects their national interest. The Sino-American relationship has been viewed with a more critical eye, particularly in view of the continuing problem of Taiwan (which the CCP leaders see as an inalienable part of their national territory) and relations with the Soviet Union have warmed, with agreements to boost trade as well as technical and economic co-operation, resulting in a more or less equidistant stance between the two superpowers.

The second and third worlds nevertheless remain the major foci of China's diplomacy, with the EC and Japan seen as crucial sources of technology and economic co-operation by the Chinese whose diplomats have of late been at pains to assert that differences in political and social systems are immaterial to their foreign relations. The deeply personalised nature of traditional Chinese political thinking has been demonstrated by their cultivation of individual political party leaders in the West, even if out of office—Britain's former Conservative Prime Minister, Edward Heath, being an obvious case in point—in addition to government leaders. But just as the Chinese refuse to be dominated by either of the superpowers, so also do they claim not to interfere in the internal affairs of other states.

Further evidence of the Chinese leaders' pragmatism has been their support for Third World countries, formerly an article of China's communist faith. The Chinese have not disavowed the need to promote revolution and back so-called national liberation movements but at the same time they pay less attention to the political complexion of Third World governments than they do to their mutual economic disadvantages in relation to the developed countries. China has continued to associate with the demands of developing nations to reform the international economic order and strengthen South-South co-operation but her leaders now share the view that a grouping and a concept which embraces nations as diverse as the wealthy OPEC states as well as poorer African countries is outmoded.

The Second World countries of the EC and Japan have much to offer China in both economic and national security terms. Japan remains in important partner but the Chinese are reluctant to rely too heavily on this source of advanced technology, especially in view of recent trade frictions; the EC, however, offers a greater diversity of supply sources, markets and political choices.

China established diplomatic relations with the EC at Community level in 1975 and although trade and economic co-operation have so far been pursued with individual countries, the Chinese leaders see this West European bloc as a growing force in international affairs and welcome trends towards its greater unity. In this vein China's Premier Zhao Ziyang, on a visit to Britain in June 1985, spoke of his country's high regard for the EC countries not only as important economic and technological partners but as an important force in maintaining world peace. While individual countries have their own strengths and expertise, which may prove useful to the Chinese in their modernisation programme, the Community is greater than the sum of its parts. London is still a major financial centre but what the Chinese see as significant is Britain increasingly sharing the views of other European countries on international affairs. Whether this argument is valid or not, the Chinese may well consider Britain—along with its influence in other parts of the world—as China's bridgehead in Europe, even though other major countries like France and the Federal Republic of Germany may have other contributions to make to China's economic development.

It is what they believe is the EC's growing independence that the Chinese admire, and in their view this is in part due to its economic strength: in 1979 Western Europe surpassed the USA in terms of national income, for example, total foreign trade and steel output. Moreover, the Chinese regarded the contest in military strength between the two superpowers as more and more unfavourable to the USA, thereby rendering the American protective umbrella over Western Europe less effective. Thus, although reporting favourably on European peace movements, the Chinese media praised the European Parliament's resolution which, in addition to studying the political, economic and social problems of the Community, enabled it to discuss questions of European security, indicating a greater reliance on the Community's own armed strength to defend its interests and safety.[1]

Certainly, as the natural gas pipeline controversy showed, EC countries could differ from the USA over how to deal with the Soviet threat. In the wake of events such as the USSR occupation of Afghanistan, the Americans considered the merits of economic sanctions against the Soviet Union. This view was not entirely shared, however, by EC countries like the Federal Republic of Germany which gave national companies the go-ahead in 1982 to supply pipeline equipment to the Soviet Union. The Siberian gas, which has been supplied to Western Europe since early 1984, provides only a small proportion of the energy needs of Austria, the Federal Republic of Germany, France and Italy, and so these countries are not completely dependent on the Soviet Union in this regard. There was a claim that as a result of this economic stake the Russians were less likely to threaten the peace and stability of Europe. Thus, there are parallels between China's new realpolitik and the EC's policy of limited economic co-operation with the Soviet Union.

If the Chinese wish to foster this independent stance of the EC countries, at the same time they do not deny the need for armed vigilance on all fronts or the desirability of defence agreements and arms contracts with the West, directed against Soviet power. Although American sales of helicopters, coastal defence radar, communications equipment and other military *matériel* to China have often overshadowed European initiatives, the Chinese have sought EC expertise, as in the technical and industrial co-operation agreement with Italy in early 1985. This was in two parts: the supply of defence systems and the exchange of military personnel. Military hardware purchased by China includes such items as radar systems and interceptor planes. But more significant are the provisions for training Chinese military personnel in areas like flight control and highly specialised aeronautics knowhow.[2] The scale of strategic goods or those with possible military application is still inhibited by the embargo applied to Communist countries by the leading Western industrial nations, but China could prove a lucrative market for European military supplies, even though China exports smaller weapons. For the time being, however, the Chinese are likely to buy goods like machinery and plant directly related to their modernisation programme, economic development being seen as a prerequisite for national defence. Similarly, the Chinese leaders see the achievement of economic viability as the main challenge facing the Third World.

Japan, like China, though for other reasons and with different perspectives, is embarked upon a more independent foreign policy, under pressure both from nationalist feeling in Japan and other members of the Western alliance. Even prior to World War II, the Japanese had built a sound industrial base, and until the military ascendancy of the 1930s the formation of cabinets led by leaders of political parties pointed to limited forms of representative government. Defeat in war brought an Allied occupation which was for all intents and purposes an American one and, since the movement of individuals in and out of Japan was closely monitored, the US authorities (under General MacArthur) were able to set about a transformation of Japanese society in 'laboratory' conditions—the main aim being to eradicate the hierarchical authoritarian patterns of the past, instil demo-cratic ideals, and thus prevent a revival of Japanese militarism. A new political system based on British and American institutions was imposed and took root, although the political process within the institutional framework has been informed by traditional social patterns such as group loyalty and consensus decision-making.

In seeking to create a peace-loving Japan which would never again threaten its neighbors, the Occupation authorities put in the 1946 Constitution the anti-war clause, Article IX, which for-bade the maintenance of war potential, even denying the Japa-nese the right of self defence. By the late 1940s, however, in the wake of the Cold War, Occupation policy had shifted from reform to emphasis on rehabilitation, and Japan was enlisted as a bastion against communism in Asia. The para-military forces originally meant for internal policing have become a conventional army, air force, and navy organised against attack from outside. The events of Hiroshima and Nagasaki and the inclusion of Article IX in the Constitution had, however, combined to produce strong pacifist sentiments which successive Japanese governments have had to take into account in acceding to post-war US demands for Japan to rearm and shoulder a greater defence burden. While approaches of Japanese Prime Ministers to this issue of rearma-ment have varied, in general they have acceded only slowly to American demands while sheltering under US Defence treaties on the assumption that any kind of attack on Japan would meet with a response from America. While Japanese governments have given Article IX a moral rather than a strictly legal interpretation to justify the maintenance of armed forces, they have so far refused to use them in action overseas, thus allaying South-east Asian suspicions of Japanese motives in the region. A cardinal principle of Japanese foreign policy has been that economic stability is the best guarantee of political stability—and thus defence—with regard to both Japan and the Asian region as a whole. Not surprisingly, however, high economic growth and export surpluses have led to charges that Japan has not pulled her weight in defence expenditure and has enjoyed a free ride on the backs of American taxpayers.

From 1976 to 1985 a ceiling of one percent of national income was placed on defence spending. In 1985 Prime Minister Naka-sone took a different stance from most of his predecessors and lifted this ceiling to allow an expansion of Japan's military capability. This was certainly in response to American calls for

Japan to take more responsibility for the defence of Asia and the Pacific, and to soothe US apprehension over Japanese export offensives but it also reflects public concern in Japan itself about the increased Soviet naval presence and general military build-up in the North Pacific. Opinion polls in the 1980s have similarly indicated a greater public acceptance of Japan's Self-Defence Forces, despite doubts about their constitutional legitimacy.

In Japan's Defence Build-Up Plan from 1986 to 1990, the one percent limit is being slightly exceeded and this will increase the already formidable capability of the country's armed forces in an Asian context. The major objectives of the 1986–90 Plan are (i) to enhance Japan's ability to defend its air space and protect its vital sea lanes, and to be able to engage in combat in coastal waters and beyond; (ii) command operations are to be improved and communications systems updated through the use of communications satellites; (iii) the capacity to engage in sustained conflict is to be increased.[3] Greater acceptance of the need for more defence spending among both the leaders of the ruling Liberal Democratic Party (LDP) and the Japanese public, however, comes as much from heightened awareness of Japan's exposed strategic position in Northeast Asia as from the prompting of Western allies. Like certain countries of the EC, Japan must face the reality of Soviet military power close at hand: some doubts, whether justified or not, may also be felt as to whether the American defence umbrella over Japan could or would prove effective in the event of a world-wide conflict between the West and the Soviet Union.

Certainly, Japanese perceptions of the Soviet military build-up—for example, on the disputed Kurile Islands, just north of Japan—have convinced recent Japanese governments of the crucial need for greater military preparedness. Like West Germany and China, Japan has irredenta with the Soviet Union. At least some of the islands of the Kurile Chain (like Etorofu as well as Habomai and Shikotan, located but a few kilometres from the coast of Japan's northernmost territory of Hokkaido) are indisputably Japanese in historical and legal terms but were occupied by the Soviets after World War II and the subsequent treaties. The Soviet leaders are unwilling to return the islands to Japan lest a precedent be set leaving the way open for claims from China which lost territory in central Asia taken from a weak Chinese dynasty by Tsarist rulers in the mid-nineteenth century, not to mention similar demands from European states. The Soviet military have also established surveillance installations on the Kuriles to monitor United States naval movements in the Pacific.

In view of this proximity of Soviet military power, any independent Japanese defence and foreign policy is still mapped firmly within the framework of the alliance with the USA. The Asia-Pacific region is of crucial importance to the USA both in terms of defence and as a supplier of raw materials, especially for America's new industrial sectors like electronics and space navigation industries: thus 97 percent of the titanium and 82 percent of the tin imported by the USA come from the Asia-Pacific region. Furthermore, in recent years there has been a significant shift in the pattern of America's regional trade. While, from the end of World War II until 1975, Western Europe was the USA's major trading partner, by 1982 its share was only a little over 25 percent compared with Pacific region's share of nearly 35 percent.[4] For these reasons the USA is likely to maintain and strengthen its commitments in the area while calling upon allies like Japan to play a greater role in their own defence. US troops in the region already account for about a third of American forces stationed abroad. Thus while increasing their own military strength, defence collaboration with Japan is being consolidated. The Japanese have now been given the tasks of controlling the Soya, Tsugaru, and Tsushima Straits through which Soviet ships must pass to move southwards, as well as defending 1,000 nautical mile seaways close to Japan.[5] The Japanese are deploying an all-weather monitoring system in order to track Soviet vessels passing through the Soya Strait, a method as effective as the old radar system. Similarly, the USA and Japan agreed in October 1982 to station 50 F-16 fighter planes (capable of carrying both conventional and nuclear weapons) at Misawa, 560 kilometres north-west of Tokyo and about 700 kilometres south of the Soviet military base on the island of Sakhalin.

But while the Soviet threat demands armed vigilance on the part of Japan, it does not preclude economic co-operation between the two countries in ways similar to European initiatives. This economic relationship has nevertheless been inhibited in various respects by historical antecedents and the current configuration of power in Northeast Asia. In 1956 the Japanese established diplomatic relations and signed a Peace Agreement, though not a peace treaty, with the Soviet Union, and the absence of a peace treaty hinders progress in economic co-operation. The Japanese have stated categorically that there can be no treaty without the return of the Northern territories; the Soviet leaders deny the legitimacy of Japan's claim.

Economic co-operation could bring mutual benefit, and there are increasing signs of moves in this direction. Soviet economic development has been concentrated in European Russia but natural resources in these areas may well be exhausted by the turn of the century and so future growth could depend much more on the raw materials and forests in Siberia and the Far East, areas which are also of great strategic significance. In fact, in the Far East Russia has about one third of its armed services and sited nuclear weapons like SS-20 missiles. Both economic development and military strength in this region nevertheless depend on the creation of a viable infrastructure, such as a transportation network. In logistical terms it is more sensible for Russia to call on Japanese expertise which is close at hand than to transport machinery and equipment from European Russia. Japan, on the other hand, is short of commodities like energy and timber, and Siberia could meet some of its needs. Even in a world of falling prices and an oil glut, the diversification of suppliers by Japan is still sought in view of the volatile politics of the Middle East. Co-operative arrangements with Russia in the exploitation of resources were being made in the 1970s but several projects were subsequently stymied by such factors as the different nature of the two economic systems: Soviet reluctance to divulge sensitive information required in surveys and problems in agreeing about returns on investment were cases in point. Negotiations held between the two governments in 1986 resulted in only tentative expressions of intent on economic and territorial issues, but economic co-operation is a likely option for the future, with the Japanese considering agreements in this field in a way similar to the EC view on the gas pipeline. Given periodic trade frictions between Japan and the USA the Soviet Union (in addition to the EC countries) promises a lucrative alternative market and a fruitful field of investment.

In the general context of international relations, then, the Chinese and the Japanese have increasingly sought to pursue independent foreign policies. In this sense their relations with EC countries are comparable. China–EC and Japan–EC economic relations, however, are better contrasted: Japan has become a formidable rival for the countries of Western Europe; China is yet to make a real impact there.

Japan's phenomenal post-war economic growth calls for examination at this point since factors contributing to it may have an important bearing on the country's relations with Western Europe in the future. Initially, a world abundance of raw materials—at least until the early 1970s—a rapid expansion of world trade and developments in international relations aided Japan's economic recovery so that industrial production levels soon reached and exceeded their pre-war peaks. The American Occupation provided a period of stability and a defence umbrella; coinciding with and furthering economic 'take-off' were requisitions from Japan for the US forces in the Korean War during 1950-52. These factors alone, however, do not account for the Japanese ability to sustain economic growth, and by the 1980s to attain the second highest national income in the free world. In contrast with other Asian societies, where traditional social values appear to have impeded modernisation, Japanese traits such as group loyalty, obedience to superiors, and consensus decision-making actually helped to promote economic development. Social cohesion was shown, for instance, in smooth labour-management relations and a unique relationship between government and big business. Although Japan's has been a free market economy, government intervention (for example, in the automobile industry) has often helped restructuring to take account of trends in world trade. In the 1960s and 1970s, government officials and business leaders got together to advise on research and development, staking out new areas in which the economy could become competitive. Patents and licenses acquired from US companies had earlier hastened the adoption and improvement of the best technology from abroad, thus obviating the need to spend on research during this period. By the 1970s, however, co-ordination between government and business and increased expenditure by companies as well as the government on research and development all helped to make Japan the leader in fields like information technology and robotics. Japan the pupil became Japan the mentor.

The government also protected 'infant' industries and through tariffs insulated them from foreign competition. A high rate of personal saving by the Japanese enabled banks to lend funds for the expansion of industry. Thus a buoyant domestic market (for, say, new consumer goods) became well-established before entering foreign markets, and by the later 1960s exports began to play a much bigger role in the Japanese economy. Moreover, during the early post-war years, Japanese industrial wages remained low enough to give Japan's exports a price advantage though this was also helped by high productivity.

By the late 1960s, however, Japanese exports of goods such as textiles and even electronics were facing competition from the newly industrialising countries of Asia like Taiwan and South Korea. The Japanese accordingly began to move into other sectors and are still proving singularly adept at restructuring the economy, according to trends in world trade. Similarly, by the 1980s emphasis was shifting from 'smokestack' industries like steel and chemicals to knowledge-intensive ones. Such is the quality of Japanese consumer goods that they have flooded EC markets; even Japanese agreement to voluntary quotas has failed to meet the concern of European leaders about the survival of their own industries.

But while a powerful trade rival of the advanced industrial countries, Japan is nevertheless vulnerable to stoppages in sources of supply, as the bulk of her energy and raw materials are imported. The greatest economic power in the world, the USA, is Japan's foremost trading partner, and original Japanese moves into European markets were partly in response to American protectionist pressures. In addition, precisely because Japan has so often bought American natural resources in exchange for manufactured goods—a vertical trade relationship—the US authorities have enjoyed more leverage with the Japanese than have their national counterparts in EC countries.

Aware of their vulnerability, the Japanese are seeking to avoid the growing danger of European protectionist barriers by exporting capital and investing in production facilities in EC countries. Individual EC countries benefit from increased employment, investment and new skills; the Japanese hope then to reach markets in other EC states more readily. Thus Japan, though a latecomer to the industrial revolution, has surpassed the West in some areas of research and development, and Japanese investment may well assist EC countries in their industrial restructuring. Equally, there is scope for European industrial leaders to engage in joint ventures in Japan. Consequently, the EC-Japan economic relationship may be called horizontal since the same kinds of manufactured goods are exchanged, technology is transferred, and joint ventures in similar economic sectors promoted in each of the two countries.

China, like Japan, entered the post-war world in a state of economic devastation but the nature and scale of her problems have been vastly different. At the Communist accession in 1949 the Chinese economy was still largely based on subsistence agriculture with about 80 percent of the population deriving their livelihood from the land. The Chinese Communist leaders were dedicated to creating an advanced industrial China but their difficulties were compounded by a shortage of qualified scientific and technical personnel. Moreover, much of China's industry was concentrated on the coast and in the Northeastern provinces, the greater part of it developed by foreign enterprise in the Treaty Ports (formerly leased by colonial powers). In the short term, China's economy could only be rebuilt by massive amounts of foreign assistance. Earlier misunderstandings with the Western powers precluded aid from countries like the USA which was then helping to rebuild war-torn Europe, and the Chinese Communists turned to the Soviet leaders with whom they shared the Marxist-Leninist ideology. Soviet assistance was not especially generous—perhaps because the Russians were reluctant to have a rival for themselves in the international Communist movement—and was in any case in the form of credits and loans rather than outright aid. Where the Chinese did benefit was in the despatch to China of Soviet technical specialists who put their expertise to work on projects based on Soviet blueprints. Extensive literacy programmes were started in China to further political control and facilitate skill acquisition, while large numbers of students were sent to be trained in Soviet institutes.

Not surprisingly, the economic strategy adopted was essentially Soviet; in the First Five Year Plan, for example, stress was placed on heavy industry (with less investment allocated to agriculture which was nevertheless required to feed a growing population), providing raw materials for light industry and producing exports to pay for imports of capital equipment. By the end of the First Five Year Plan in 1957, however, it had become apparent that slow growth in agriculture was impeding progress in other sectors, since resources available for exports in order to buy imports were heavily dependent on the harvest of the preceding year. Certain aspects of Soviet central planning were proving to be unsuited to Chinese conditions, and as the Sino-Soviet dispute intensified, Communist leaders turned to their own revolutionary tradition in their search for a solution to economic problems. Accordingly, the strategy was modified in subsequent Five Year Plans. In 1958 Mao Zedong launched the ill-fated Great Leap forward, involving a policy of national self-reliance, decentralisation of administration, some ad hoc planning as well as social mobilisation measures to create economic take-off and self-sufficiency in local areas, with less disbursement of funds from the central treasury. The communes—which evolved from amalgamating the earlier collectives in the countryside, though with strong ecouragement from the Communist Party—encompassed not only agricultural activities but also extensive public works and local industries, (using China's abundant rural labour force in slack seasons). Communes also took over local government administration with responsibilities for services like education and health.

But this attempt to generate rapid economic growth in the rural areas, especially regarding agriculture, was not successful; after the announcement of high grain yields in 1958, later admitted to have been exaggerated, a series of bad harvests followed. In addition, materials like iron and steel produced by makeshift processes often proved unusable, and local leaders had clearly moved too far and too fast in trying to follow directives and impress higher authorities. By the early 1960s a retreat from the more ambitious features of the Great Leap Forward was being sounded, with the peasants being allowed to cultivate private plots—representing a small percentage of the collective land area—for commercial gain; produce was allowed to be sold on the revived system of rural market fairs to provide incentives for the peasants to grow vegetables, for example, and thereby alleviating shortages in the cities. Decentralisation within the commune was also carried out and greater initiative given to the smaller agricultural units, the production teams and brigades; the former, however, retained the administration of local government.

In a sense, the Chinese had made a virtue out of necessity; to a great extent they were compelled to be self-reliant in view of the withdrawal of Soviet assistance, experts and blueprints. The Great Leap had also taught the leadership important lessons: while the creation of rural industries introduced some new skills, the Chinese could not afford to neglect agriculture which could not progress far without further technological inputs and investment; and in busy seasons, at least, available labour should not be drawn away to other activities.

While the communes were a rural phenomenon, the fervour of the Great Leap affected other sectors. The Chinese leaders had all along believed that economic development could be achieved through ideological incentives, that is to say, by arousing the work-force and the population in general to greater efforts even if funding and technology were insufficient. Certainly, growth had been helped along by the improvisation of the old pre-war repair shops and, more importantly, by the industrial plant the Soviets had introduced, but it was becoming apparent by the mid-1960s that further advances required the latest world-level technology to be imported. Accordingly, in the late 1960s, as trade with the Communist bloc fell, that with Japan and Western Europe rose. With the death of Mao Zedong and the political rehabilitation of leading figures (like Deng Xiaoping, China's current elder statesman) who had been disgraced because of their advocacy of more pragmatic policies, China was opened up to the outside world; trade with the West increased and economic co-operation invited.

To Western traders China at last seemed a vast market eldorado, and while such hopes are yet to be fully realised, there are opportunities for much more trade and economic co-operation.

But is it in the interests of EC countries to help build up China's economy? Could she be a trade competitor in years to come? Moreover, will the greater military potential made possible by increased economic strength prove a threat to peace? The Chinese leaders have never forsworn support for world revolution, and China's economic reforms do not appear to have significantly weakened the dictatorship of the Communist Party. But modernisation will be a long process, and China's elder statesman, Deng Xiaoping, and his associates justify economic co-operation with the West in terms of improving the living standards of the Chinese people—on which they have staked their own political legitimacy and, by implication, that of their successors. In January 1987, in view of Hu Yaobang's relinquishing the post of General Secretary of the CCP, there were signs of a 'conservative' (in China, read 'leftist') backlash, but it seems unlikely as yet that Deng's economic reforms—including concessions to market forces—will be completely reversed. Rising expectations, especially in relation to consumer goods and other trappings of the good life in China, will make the economic reforms difficult to reverse. As China's wealth increases, she will become a 'have' power with a vested interest in the existing international economic system. This could dictate political choices and thus reduce Chinese enthusiasm for world revolution and military adventures. It may therefore be to the EC's advantage to promote China's economic self-interest. However successful the Chinese are in using and improving upon Western technology, it will be many years before China becomes, for the EC, a rival of Japan's stature. The next chapter will examine the question of China's receptivity to foreign investment and technology by looking at the on-going reform of the Chinese economy; the following chapter will then examine the nature and extent of China's trade and economic co-operation with the EC.

2
The Reform of China's Economic System

The Third Plenum of the Eleventh Central Committee of the Chinese Communist Party, one of China's major ruling bodies, held in December 1978, was a watershed in the politics of contemporary China. At that session China's elder statesman, Deng Xiaoping, emerged as the country's most powerful political figure and helped to launch the Four Modernisations: of agriculture, industry, science and technology and national defence. These involved a thoroughgoing programme of economic reform. At subsequent high Communist Party meetings during the following two years, a number of officials who had been disgraced during the Cultural Revolution were publicly and politically rehabilitated, and Deng Xiaoping was then able to place his main supporters in key government positions. Simultaneously also, Mao Zedong's contribution to the Chinese Communist revolution was reassessed; while he had formulated the political and military strategy to gain power and laid the foundations in the 1950s for later economic advance, his stress on mass mobilisation and ideological incentives to achieve development goals, as in the Great Leap Forward, and his social experiments—like mass participation in decision-making, the hallmark of the Cultural Revolution—caused deep divisions in Chinese society, bequeathing a legacy of political factionalism and setting China's progress back a generation.

This reassessment has had wide-ranging implications for China's domestic and foreign policies. Although Mao Zedong rejected China's Confucian heritage, much of his political thinking bore the imprint of traditional notions of social and political control, especially in connection with the educability of each individual who could thereby be transformed into the new Communist man or woman. In traditional China the state was conceived of as the extension of society, with filial piety within families and among friends being analogies for the relationship between Emperor and subject. Such clearly defined rules of conduct made

28

the individual subordinate to the group. This subordination on a social level was also reinforced in economic terms; Imperial China was ruled by a bureaucracy of scholar officials, recruited on the basis of merit by an examination in the Confucian classics. Moreover, because the merchant occupied the lowest position in the social hierarchy, and any centres of independent economic power were in some way controlled by government, all avenues to high status in society were political. In addition, while traditional China did not lack scientific and technical invention, social values were not conducive to their development, and this has been proposed as the reason for the lack of an industrial revolution in China until the Western impact in the mid-nineteenth century. Thus to the extent that the acquisitive instinct—the epitome of entrepreneurship—developed in China, it did so in a hostile environment. Even in Western Europe capitalism, together with laws concerning the sanctity of property and civil liberties, are comparatively recent phenomena and only emerged over a period of centuries.

Against this background, all nineteenth and twentieth-century Chinese reformers and revolutionaries have sought to create a new ideology, replacing Confucianism and the old political institutions it has sanctioned, in order to further the two objectives of nationalism and modernisation. China has never had a tradition of representative government as understood in the West, and having themselves been brought up in authoritarian social and political values, the Chinese Communists turned to Marxism-Leninism, which Mao Zedong, the leader of the C.C.P., adapted to Chinese conditions. As with its adoption elsewhere in the Third World, Chinese Marxism-Leninism has had a strong anti-imperialist component and its command economy was seen initially, at least, as a shortcut to rapid development. The freedom sought for the nation, from alleged semi-colonisation, was not extended to the individual who remained subservient to the Communist Party, even though the latter claimed, as the vanguard of the proletariat, to speak in the name of the people.

In opening their country to the outside world and seeking to encourage foreign trade and investment, Deng Xiaoping and his supporters have tried to reassure the Westerners of the safety of their stake in the Chinese economy. They have tried also to convince the Chinese people of the need for changes in attitude if China is to benefit from foreign contact and be receptive to technology from overseas. Thus, even though they have no wish to abandon socialism nor to relinquish state control over the

economy, international trade competition demands that some room be given to market forces at home, and these require a degree of private entrepreneurship and the values associated with it. Given that the Chinese Communist Party is, in the Marxist-Leninist view, the repository of revolutionary wisdom, it must justify these changes of policy in ideological terms. In September 1984 a Chinese theoretical journal carried an article explaining that China's feudal period had lasted much longer than Europe's; China had thus missed the individualist phase, moving into socialism via semi-colonialism and semi-feudalism, thus missing a period of developed capitalism.[1] China had exchanged one brand of collectivism for another.

Two factors contributed to attitudes unfavourable to entrepreneurship and individual initiative. While some of the CCP's leaders came from the ranks of the old educated classes, the Party's major base on its road to power had been the peasantry, and under Mao it became essentially anti-intellectual. In addition, the exigencies of revolutionary war placed a premium on practical experience and technical improvisation rather than academic excellence. Although during the period from 1949 to 1976 large numbers of scientists and technical experts were trained, they were periodically subjected to thought-reform campaigns designed to instil loyalty to the Communist regime, and politics was uppermost. In the long term, this policy towards intellectuals and managers proved a recipe for backwardness; leaders of industrial enterprises had to work within the state plan and had virtually no scope for initiative in matters like output levels, product specialisation and deployment of the work-force. As a result, with the onset of the post-1976 reforms, old habits have died hard with management, even when given the initiative, being reluctant to innovate lest the political line from above should change.

To the outside observer Chinese economic policies suffered in the past from a surfeit of dogma. Though still claiming to adhere to Marxist-Leninist theory, Deng Xiaoping and his associates have enjoined others to 'seek truth from facts', that is to say, the test of any measure lies in its results. Quotations from Lenin have been cited to emphasise that the so-called struggle between dying capitalism and developing socialism is concrete and not abstract—in other words, the effectiveness of reform will lie in its ability to raise China's standard of living.

Thus traditional Chinese socio-political values and too rigid an adherence to Marxist-Leninist dogma are seen as impediments to economic progress. In fact, however, although stages of development differ, policy debates in China are not so very different from those currently taking place in the Western world. The question is not whether but the extent to which the state or central government should play a role in the national economy and other areas which impinge upon the freedom of the individual. As in many other countries, the state in China will take responsibility for basic services like welfare, health and education but current reforms envisage the national administration withdrawing from decision-making in enterprise management; hitherto, the allocation of investment, the setting of output targets and the distribution of products were controlled by the central government. The central government will, of course, remain in charge of national defence and co-ordinate the activities and interests of local governments, enterprises and the community at large.

The Chinese economic reforms will initially be discussed within the context of the Communist bloc. In introducing a new economic measure the Chinese Communists, both before and after 1976, adopted the technique of experimenting with measures over a limited geographical area and then extending them to the whole country. Thus the agricultural responsibility system—which broke up the People's Communes and involved contracting with individual households—was first developed in Anhui Province in 1979. Similarly, changes in industrial management practices were first tried out in Shanghai and the Southwestern Province of Sichuan in the early 1980s. In having no overall blueprint for reform, China comes close to the Soviet approach. Nevertheless, in adopting a more open economic policy and trying to raise production efficiency with the specific aim of making export goods competitive, the Chinese measures have greater affinity with Hungarian reforms.[2]

It has often been said that the most dangerous moment for a despotism is when it begins to reform and China—where economic changes in motion are in many respects more thoroughgoing than in other Communist countries—is now in a period of transition when human and material impediments are rapidly coming to the fore. Adjustments in one area of a command economy inevitably bring in their wake the need for more extensive changes in other areas. The performance of China's economy since the late 1970s will thus be assessed in the light of reform and its results to date.

The first task of Deng Xiaoping and other leaders has been

to convince cadres and those in authority at various levels of administration that reform is crucial for China's economic prosperity and that it is in everyone's best interests to support it. Arising out of traditional socio-cultural patterns—and in spite of the command economy—Chinese individuals are more influenced by personal as opposed to contractual relationships than are their Soviet and East European counterparts; they are thus more resistant to major changes. Command economies are notorious for red tape, the black market and shortages; in China in the past, in order to survive and thrive, managers and enterprises saw to their own interests—for example, by stockpiling raw materials in short supply and by developing informal networks of personal relations not amenable to control by the central government. This is a kind of corruption but certainly not private enterprise in the true sense. In a centrally-planned and state-run economy the status of civil servants and bureaucrats is derived from political privilege rather than money per se; thus they feel threatened by the institution of a market economy because they are not equipped either by training and experience or by inclination to compete in a business-orientated environment. This is why so far it has proved more difficult to apply the mechanisms of the market in industry than in agriculture where even in collectives and communes, households were responsible for production on land near their homes. In contrast, in the cities a state-run enterprise is the lowest rung of the bureaucratic ladder.[3]

Aware or not of these political constraints, China's top leaders have pressed ahead with reform. From 1976 to 1978, Hua Guofeng—formerly a little-known agricultural expert who had been named as Mao Zedong's successor, though as a compromise choice, to bridge competing factions in the Chinese Communist Party—launched an ambitious modernisation programme which, while it differed from the Maoist line in stressing a greater role for technical expertise, maintained the policy of expanding heavy industry at the expense of other sectors. In the event, however, the goals proved too ambitious, causing major dislocation and imbalances. Moreover, Hua lacked a broad base of political power and proved a temporary leader. By 1978, newly rehabilitated political figures, led by Deng Xiaoping, had rejected the old economic strategy and decided upon the promotion of more balanced growth; while there was excess, and in some cases obsolescent, heavy industrial plant in the various regions, agriculture and light industry had been relatively neglected. Agriculture was still the basis of the economy, and the Deng leadership opted for material incentives as a means of encouraging the peasantry to increase grain yields, to feed a growing population and provide raw materials for manufacturing as well as exports. Attention had simultaneously to be paid to light industry, given the need to produce consumer goods to soak up the increased income of the peasantry. Heavy industry was not neglected but its growth targets scaled down. In addition, China was critically short of energy, with adverse effects on industry, and the distribution of products was handicapped by an inadequate transportation system. These shortcomings would have to be put right if China were to use foreign technology and investment to full advantage. Indeed, Japan and the EC are already playing a part in the development of new energy resources and the provision of more physical infrastructure.

These years of readjustment from 1979 to 1981 mark the beginning of the current reform programme. By 1981 the Chinese leadership had concluded that the central planning system must be overhauled, and the following four years saw a major restructuring of agricultural organisation. While there was no intention of reverting to the old system of private land ownership, the CCP believed that the collective economy in the countryside had been consolidated, and freer rein should now be given to the entrepreneurial talents of the peasantry. In the past private plots—small areas around private dwellings—had been revived and limited sideline activities permitted, but now the peasants were to be given a greater say in the crops planted on collectively-owned land. They would also be paid more for grain produced over and above the required state quota and, if yields were increased, there could be greater scope for crop diversification. The mechanism for achieving these goals has been the contract responsibility system linking output with payment on a household basis. As implemented in one province, Anhui, from 1979 and later extended over most of the country, this reform has involved the lowest level of the former collective, the production team, consisting of thirty to forty households, making contracts with groups of a dozen of these households for certain quantities of output at state prices. After obligations to the state and the collective have been met, the remainder of the produce is at the disposal of the household for its own use, sale on the free market or sale to the state at special negotiated prices. It has been estimated that, as of 1983, 80 percent of all rural households were involved in the new system. As a further incentive, in 1984 the Chinese government raised the prices at which it purchased agricultural products. Nevertheless, however impressive grain figures in the mid-1980s may have been, they were limited to the achievement of increased yields solely on the basis of peasant initiative, without the benefit of capital and technology from higher authorities like the central government. Much investment will be required in areas like irrigation, for example, pest control, and the scientific use of fertilisers.

The encouragement of limited forms of private enterprise and crop diversification is bringing in its train other socio-economic changes. About 80 percent of China's population lives in the countryside, and ever since 1949 the cities have attracted rural people seeking better living standards and amenities. But because of unemployment in urban centres, the government discourages migration on any large scale, and envisages the creation of industry in the rural areas to soak up any excess labour. While few peasant entrepreneurs are in a position to make huge fortunes, the agricultural reforms are producing a spin-off effect because crop diversificaiton is creating great employment opportunities. It is calculated that over 52 million country-dwellers or about 14 percent of the total rural workforce are now employed in township industries rather than directly in agriculture. Plants for processing vegetables, fruit and meat, and manufacturing other agricultural products are being given high priority, and so are service industries. In addition, the government claims that there are 25 million 'specialised households' which, on the basis of private enterprise, are operating rural transport services and working in the tens of thousands of free markets across China, expanded to cope with the demands created by the agricultural reforms.[4] Per capita rural incomes are increasing both as a result of these occupational changes and peasant entrepreneurship.

The introduction of the rural responsibility system and the expansion of rural commerce have themselves fostered a greater demand among the peasantry for industrial products and technological knowhow. Consequently, strong distribution links are being created between the cities and the countryside. Given the economic strategy of balanced development outlined during the readjustment period and the Sixth Five Year Plan (1981–1985), agricultural reorganisation has been the prerequisite for the reform of industry. Prior to reform, control of agriculture had been centralised at the commune level and its products subject to unified purchase by the state; similarly, most of China's industries were nationalised—the central government allocating investment funds, distributing the goods and determining the size and nature of the work-force. In the absence of market forces, industries had guaranteed sales and, while international trade played such a minor role in China's economy, were immune from competition. Under the guidance of national plans all state enterprises fell within the jurisdiction of various central government ministries or local organs at the provincial, city, and other levels. The major problem was that business and government were separated and this did not further co-ordination, sound practice and efficiency. Innovation was also impeded by excessive dependence on the controlling authorities. Inter-ministerial infighting and the protection of bureaucratic vested interests meant little cross-fertilisation of ideas and exchange of personnel, and few joint projects. Nor were state enterprises subject only to control by government organs. In China it is the Communist Party that controls government and not vice versa and factory directors were subordinate to the party committees in decision-making. Political criteria ranked higher than technical or managerial expertise.

It was in this area of decision-making that the first tentative steps towards urban reform were taken. Such powers of decision, previously concentrated in the hands of government organs, were devolved to a hundred major industrial enterprises on an experimental basis. The central planning mechanism remained intact and initiatives given to enterprises were as yet confined only to certain aspects of production, sales and the retention of a proportion of profits. It was the first attempt by the central government to make enterprise leaders accountable for their performance through economic rather than administrative levers, the long-term implication being that inefficient operations would be closed down. By 1980 the experiment had been extended to over 6,000 enterprises. The next major watershed in the reform was the change-over from the remission of profits by enterprises to the payment of taxes on profits to the state, instituted in June 1983. For these purposes state enterprises were divided into categories: the smaller were taxed on income; the larger and medium-sized were subject to both an income tax fixed at 55 percent and the submission of a portion of profits. By October 1984, the latter had been placed on the full tax footing. These measures also required changes in certain other industrial and commercial taxes which had previously been separately levied on enterprises. Tax concessions were also given where an enterprise's revenues exceeded the profits of the reference year in which the initial assessment had been made.

At the root of these policies has been the incentive to foster initiative; high performers will be commended and the backward spurred on to greater efforts. Moreover, government intervention in the running of enterprises has been reduced as the market has come to play a key role in production plans. As in agriculture, producers still have to fulfil basic state targets and certain state contracts for the supply of goods but, having done so, may sell surpluses as well as other lines produced on their own initiative. Nevertheless, as of 1985, certain categories of industrial consumer and agricultural goods had their prices set by the state because they were of national importance.

In his May 1984 report China's Premier, Zhao Ziyang, called for more factory-director responsibilities in line with greater enterprise autonomy. As noted above, in the past Party committees, nominally responsible for political work, had in fact controlled enterprise management. At the same time as the production responsibility system was introduced, the system of factory directors assuming sole responsibility was started experimentally in 3,000 enterprises. Factory directors now had greater discretion in personnel deployment; for example, they could themselves designate staff like technicians and accountants, even if the final say still rested with government organs, and were able to hire and fire middle-level administrators on their own initiative. Promotion of employees and award of bonuses also fell within their jurisdiction. There remained some state controls on wages but these were becoming more flexible. The 'iron rice bowl' or permanent tenure of employment system was being eroded; the workforce would henceforth have an increasing stake in the health of the enterprise, and these factors in turn had implications for innovation and technical transformation.[5]

Governments in developed economies usually play a role in fostering the restructuring of old and the creation of new industries, and China will be no exception. Even under the reformed systems, only the central government can have an overall or macro-economic view. Ever since the early years of the Sino-Soviet alliance in the early 1950s, economic planning has been heavily centralised in China. But since the 1980s reforms of the planning system have been introduced with less emphasis on command type compulsory targets and more on 'guidance' through taxes, prices and finance to get enterprises to fulfil the requirements of the State Plan. At the time of writing the reforms are continuing and no conclusion as to their final implications should yet be drawn, but certain trends call for discussion. Thus, from 1985 onwards, mandatory planning was to be applied only to major industrial products like steel, chemical materials, electrical equipment and goods with military application because it was on these sectors that industries in other sectors depended.

It followed that once taxes, prices, management and personnel systems had been reformed, the financing of industry would also have to be overhauled. Since the mid-1980s investment has been increasingly financed through bank loans instead of through the system of state allocation; management is thus stimulated to improve performance.

So far discussion has been focussed on production in both agriculture and industry but this is only one part of the picture, another being that of distribution. In the past not only output but the movement of commodities was subject to central planning, with the state controlling retail and wholesale outlets. Incentives and competition in an industrial setting can only work to fullest advantage if the commercial and distribution sectors are also liberalised. Reference has already been made to rural markets where peasants are now able to sell surplus produce. Although restrictions on the sale of certain priority foods have remained, Guangzhou City, for example, deregulated vegetable transactions in November 1984, and there was no longer any obligation for producers to deliver vegetables to state-run shops. (Certain conditions, however, are still imposed to ensure a steady supply to city dwellers).[6]

Once again reform in the agricultural sphere has paved the way for changes in industry. Until the early 1980s, distribution of industrial goods was in the hands of state-owned shops. By the end of 1984, 58,000 of these had been deregulated, most to be managed collectively while still under state ownership, some to be owned and run collectively by co-operative groups and others leased to individuals. The operation of market forces meant that the old distribution system, centrally planned and involving the distribution of commodities according to regional administrative divisions, was now outmoded and being replaced by a system cutting across geographical boundaries. In addition, a number of everyday articles were derationed—cotton being one example—thus further facilitating the development of free markets.

However, there is a distinction between items for consumer

use and capital goods, and reforming the distribution system for the latter has been more complex as many of them—in view of their overriding importance for the rest of the national economy—may be subject to government procurement and allocation for some time to come. Nevertheless, distribution channels for both consumer and a few capital goods have been diversified. The province of Guangdong had been used as a pace-setter in distribution reform, and in the early 1980s the value of retail industrial goods being sold in the state-run shops was steadily declining as a proportion of the total, but in wholesale trade the stake of state shops has remained great. In the retail trade, especially in food items and in the service industries, the trend is towards leasing small state-run enterprises to individuals for personal or collective management.[7] One major aim is to make production more tailored to consumer demand.

An integral part of urban commercial reform was the trade centre concept proposed by the Central Committee of the CCP in mid-1984. Like the reforms in the field of industrial production, these measures were designed to achieve greater efficiency through incentives; management and work-force in distribution were to be given more responsibility and room for initiative. Trading centres, dealing in both consumer and some capital goods, have been opened in cities, the intention being to cut across regional boundaries. The city will thus become the matrix of distribution, with the wholesale trade as the core of the trade centre. These concepts have historical precedents: prior to the Communist accession China had a well-developed network of commercial exchange between town and country based on provincial centres.

Attempts to be more competitive on both domestic and foreign markets will be to no avail unless action is taken in the field of distribution to ensure the free flow of commodities of all kinds. By late 1984, some cities had even taken the first steps towards establishing money markets, technical fairs and labour exchanges, even though these are still subject to official guidance.

Economically, China is still in a period of transition, and the ultimate impact of ongoing agricultural and industrial reforms will be far-reaching, and their full implications, especially in the context of foreign trade and investment, considerable. It is in the nature of momentous changes that any attempt at an early judgment is soon outdated, but a preliminary assessment of progress to date is nevertheless called for. In the mid-1980s China's economic growth was impressive; in 1984, for example, industrial production grew by 13.6 percent over the previous year, the heavy sector by 13.8 percent and light industry by 13.4 percent. In the case of certain products like coal, oil and rolled steel, the targets for the Sixth Five Year Plan (1981–1985) were reached two years ahead of schedule. In 1984, 39 of the 100 key industrial products fulfilled their planned performance.

Industry's good performance in these years was due to several major factors, one of which was high investment—not least in energy sectors such as coal, oil and electricity. Energy growth was partly due to the start of oil production in the Shengli, Liaohe and Zhongyuan oilfields, and the increase in coal output (a 7.7 percent rise in 1984). A steady supply of raw materials such as steel, cement, timber and other construction materials was also a crucial factor in industrial growth, and reflected not only domestic output but imports facilitated by adequate foreign exchange reserves in 1983 and 1984. In November 1984, Vice-Premier Li Peng claimed that light and heavy industry were in balance, a goal sought by the leadership since the readjustment policies initiated in 1979–81. This was in stark contrast to earlier years of the Communist regime when consumer interests were ignored in favour of sectors like steel and machinery.

Industrial advance has often depended on a healthy agricultural sector. By the mid-1980s the two-way process of the current economic strategy was materialising: the greater income of the peasants as a result of production incentives stimulated sales of light industrial products and in turn new demand was being created for capital goods. Indeed, new sources of rural wealth were emerging in the form of construction, transportation, commerce and services. Consequently, purchasing power increased and this was in accordance with the government's encouragement of consumption. This was reflected in massive sales of electrical appliances like refrigerators, television sets, washing machines and electric fans during the mid-1980s. There was also a buoyant market for cameras and fabrics. In the wake of such incentives, agricultural production grew in 1984 by between 7 and 8 percent, with food production reaching over 400 million tons, the highest total ever. In 1983 both cereal grains and raw cotton exceeded the Sixth Five Year Plan targets.

To a large extent this success was due to the production responsibility system which covered more than 90 percent of the peasantry by 1983. As in industry, earnings increased as the central government raised the prices it paid for agricultural goods. Moreover, as intended, 'specialised households' increased in number and enjoyed high incomes, some of which were undreamed of even by high-ranking Party officials, let alone the average worker on the land or in the city factory. Success was also shown by agricultural exports which amounted to US $5.5 billion in 1984, equivalent to 20 percent of China's export earnings, and less grain was imported too. By the mid-1980s, manufactures were also playing an increasing role in exports, the outcome of economic restructuring and the growing competitiveness of Chinese goods.[8]

Economic progress, however, has not been without social cost which has serious implications for the credibility of the current leadership and, by extension, China's political stability. In spite of the absence of civil liberties and other social freedoms that are taken for granted in the West, China's command economy has in certain respects been comfortable for the Chinese on account of its predictability; thus, the allocation of resources and distribution of goods by the state could guarantee high employment and price stability. Market forces may increase efficiency and promote technological changes but they are already widening income differentials and creating more social inequalities. Competition brings prosperity but it can also cause bankruptcies and unemployment. Chinese entrepreneurs new to the market-place do not always see the less acceptable face of enterprise; they are like the inexperienced investors in stocks and shares who do not realise that prices can go down as well as up. The CCP is creating rising expectations and the economy may not grow quickly enough to satisfy them. At the root of the economic reforms is the assumption that wealth must be created before it can be distributed, and for the foreseeable future, Maoist egalitarian goals are being set aside for the demands of a developing economy. Compared with other parts of China, the coastal areas and the major cities are already advantaged in terms of investment, public amenities and natural factors and they are likely to grow even richer in the years to come. In spite of unemployment Beijing is attracting migrants seeking jobs as construction workers or domestic servants, and a high proportion of foodstuffs in Beijing's markets are sold by farmers from other provinces.[9]

Unanimity within China's current leadership is fragile and 'conservative Marxists'—some of whom still share Mao Zedong's vision of an egalitarian society—only grudgingly accept the reforms of Deng Xiaoping and his supporters. Social discontent like the student demonstrations at Beijing University in 1985 and, perhaps more significantly, the more extensive outbursts in major cities in early 1987, provide dissenting leaders with ammunition to fire at the reformers. The current leadership has enjoined the Chinese people to 'seek truth from facts', success being the test of reform. But success brings its problems, and the view is expressed that reforms have gone too far and too fast and have been undertaken at the expense of social discipline: the obsession of the young with materialism and foreign consumer goods and their neglect of social duties are seen as cases in point. Nor are rising expectations held only in material terms; enthusiasm for Western consumer goods has been followed by demands, particularly among the educated young, for those democratic freedoms enjoyed by their contemporaries in the West. The conservative Marxists believe the remedy for what they call 'cultural pollution' lies in greater political education through Marxist-Leninist teachings in the schools and universities together with a tighter rein on foreign contacts and influence within China.

To blunt the criticism of the opposition within the leadership, the reformers like Deng Xiaoping may be forced to intervene to guarantee minimum standards of living for those who are less able to look after themselves. The reform policies, however, are also open to attack on economic grounds, and potentially harmful trends have been evident; if not closely monitored, they may fall outside the government's control.

In 1985, for example, it had become clear that high growth was being achieved at the cost of inflation, a budgetary deficit and an adverse foreign trade balance. While private enterprise was being encouraged and greater decision-making powers given to state industries, both government and managers were as yet not entirely familiar with the workings of the market mechanism. In all economies governments exercise administrative controls of one kind or another and China is no exception; indeed it has been advocated that certain control instruments should be strengthened. Yet one of the main reasons for overheating in the mid-1980s was that some aspects of the command economy had been reformed and not others; prices of domestic raw materials and natural resources, essential to most sectors of industry, were not realistic. Thus success in achieving higher output has not always been accompanied by effective management at the macro-economic or government level. This factor, however, has been used as an argument not for the reversal but for the extension of reform, even though limited retrenchment policies were implemented in 1985 (and discussed later on). With the replacement of state allocation of funds to industry by a system of loans through the banking system in 1984 and 1985, there followed an excessive borrowing of funds and their misuse by enterprises, and the use of extra-budgetary bank loans and independent funds was in part responsible for the overheating of the economy. Not only did expenditure on capital construction and development of new production processes vastly increase in the pursuit of profits but funds were often misused as schemes were launched to cash in on the lucrative market for luxuries at the expense of satisfying the demand for necessities. Using their new powers, enterprises also raised the wages of their workforce, often disregarding production and profit levels; in line with the egalitarian tradition of the command economy, they distributed bonuses all round rather than rewarding individual performance. As a result, wages in the mid-1980s were rising faster than productivity. Moreover, when in 1984 the government announced measures to curb excessive wage increases and base total wage ceilings for state enterprises on current figures, some businesses immediately raised salaries—presumably to hold on to their employees—thus defeating the object of the exercise. They could afford to do this on account of the consumption boom, a reaction to the low-income syndrome of pre-reform days. As the population at large became more exposed to Western goods and life-styles, demand soared: it was a vicious circle—as wages rose to provide incentives, more money went into circulation, but the desire for goods could not be satisfied either in quantity or, more especially, quality. There was too much money chasing too few goods. Reforms of the state purchasing system meant that prices for some raw materials could be negotiated and manufacturers could bid for them when they were in short supply. Higher costs, though, meant lower profits from products which had to be sold on the domestic market because they were not competitively priced for export. Moreover, shortages led to the import of more raw materials, finished steel, lumber, chemicals and synthetic textile materials. Trade deficits of US $1.1 billion and US $14 billion ensued in 1984 and 1985.

Competition in the industrial field spurred capital construction so that productive capacity could be increased, and this resulted in a greater demand for equipment and building materials. Processing industries expanded on the basis of borrowed funds, at the same time putting pressure on energy, transport and raw materials. In 1984 and 1985, increases in energy production failed to keep pace with demand, being only about half the rate of industrial growth. In the past, too little power had forced factories to close for a part of each week.[10] China's railway system was inadequate and low freight charges resulted in other forms of transportation being used less, and bottle-necks occurred in the movement of coal and other key industrial products: in late 1985 it was reported that 50 million tons of coal were held up in the Northwest awaiting transport.

These human and physical impediments to rational well-balanced growth pointed to the perils of reforming only certain aspects of the command economy. They were not a justification for a reversal of policy but a mandate for more extensive restructuring. But it is easier to change institutional arrangements than values and habits of mind; many economic planners and managers, even as late as the mid-1980s, were still used to thinking in terms of a command economy and centralised control rather than market forces and the profit motive. In addition, the reforms of the early 1980s had paid little attention to the pricing structures of some raw materials which were out of line with the market-place; by 1984 subsidies—though sometimes disguised—were becoming increasingly out of place in a more competitive industrial setting. There is a continuing argument in favour of the State keeping a check on the prices of essential natural resources which determine growth in other major sectors but central government controls must be flexible enough to take account of technological changes affecting the exploitation and use of raw materials. For example, as coal seams have been worked and deposits depleted, mining—in the absence of modern technology—has become more expensive. Only where new machinery has been introduced have costs fallen. In 1984, however, the prices that enterprises were paying for coal had not been raised and were unrealistic, and similarly in the cases of iron ore and oil. Thus, low prices of coal led to huge wastage; despite frequent shortages, there was little incentive for industry to be cost-efficient with regard to fuel. Inefficient enterprises like small chemical fertiliser plants were being set up on the basis of cheap energy costs. In other more modern sectors, however, like electronics, chemical fibres and plastics (where the technological input is greater), prices of goods such as watches, electric fans, sewing machines and bicycles—often fixed as early as the 1950s and 1960s—remained high even though production costs had fallen.

Most of these trends in 1984 and 1985 were inflationary. In 1979 the government had increased substantially the state procurement prices for agricultural products but found it politically expedient to hold down urban consumer prices for farm produce and to subsidise the difference. This proved a drain on the State treasury.

A command economy is one of shortages and potentially inflation, even though price rises may be controlled or disguised—and the inflation may be suppressed, not open. If free rein is to be given to market forces, prices must be allowed to be determined by supply and demand. In 1985 the first steps towards corrective measures were taken, the main focus being on prices and wages. The market mechanism was to be allowed to operate; lower production costs should be reflected in lower prices for industrial goods and, in the event of more expensive raw materials and minerals, improved efficiency would offset higher costs. Prices were also adjusted in agriculture and in 1985 the unified purchase and distribution system for grain and cotton was discontinued. Instead state commercial organs were to enter into contracts with peasants on the basis of the estimated need for the coming year and at harvest time, purchase the required amount at pre-set prices. Extra output would be sold by producers on the open market. The state was to pay the fixed price for 30 percent of the contracted output but to buy the remaining 70 percent at a preferential price, that is to say, at 50 percent more than the former price. Producers were free to sell surpluses (or non-contracted) output on the open market where flexible prices obtained. The state nevertheless undertook to purchase surpluses at the fixed price if market levels fell below it. In essence, the central authorities sought to preserve incentives for peasant producers but simultaneously to prevent an excessive drain on state finances. For similar reasons, in early 1985 subsidies on pork, vegetables and other non-staple foods in Beijing and 29 other major cities were removed, the argument being that prices would find their own realistic level. These measures, however, were not applied to food grains or edible oils, but higher productivity could in time allow the remaining subsidies to be removed.

Likewise measures were introduced to rationalise coal prices which could now be raised according to quality and output. As a result negotiated prices, usually above the ones set by government, became increasingly important. Provinces that were not self-sufficient in coal were allowed to charge higher prices for locally-mined coal.[11]

While the central authorities wished to retain some control

over the allocation of essential materials, fuel and production goods required under state plans, the prices of these goods, when allowed to be sold freely by enterprises, were permitted to fluctuate. Prices of less important goods were also liberalised.[12]

Attempts were also made to reduce transportation bottle-necks by using roads and coastal waterways rather than the overloaded railways. To this end short-distance rail haulage rates were raised and regional variations in transport charges permitted.

Thus market forces were as far as possible to govern prices. In addition wage reforms were designed to reflect payment according to an individual's work performance. The independent decision-making powers regarding pay given to enterprises since the early 1980s had been abused; the old egalitarian tradition had died hard and wages had risen dramatically. In reasserting control, the central authorities placed the funds of state enterprises and government organs under the supervision of the banks. A ban was placed on the use of production development funds for bonuses. State-run bodies were to institute a new wage system designed to link a worker's income with specific job performance and the profitability of the enterprise; similar arrangements applied to civil servants. Thus wage differentials between different categories of the work-force were to be encouraged although the margins should not be too great. However, the pay of those in private-sector employment, though representing only an estimated 2.5 percent of urban employment, were less amenable to control by the central government.[13]

The Chinese leaders have made money-making respectable and, staking their legitimacy on raising China's standard of living, are unlikely to reverse the domestic reforms and open-door policies which have already brought tangible gains in terms of economic growth. The risk lies in expectations of material prosperity rising too quickly. In 1985 the elimination of subsidies on many food items and the associated price rises—together with the postponement of further wage rises in the cities—were a source of potential discontent. The direction of the Chinese leaders' corrective measures in 1986 meant that they saw the answer in higher productivity which alone could justify higher wages. The task of implementation, however, falls on the shoulders of enterprise management, now no longer able to shelter under centrally-planned low targets and job security but accountable to the work-force and its material expectations. Nevertheless, in 1986 the state still played a major role in distributing key resources to industry; it was clear, too, that increased productivity would rest not only on incentives but on technological inputs by the central government in areas such as the infrastructure, irrigation and mechanisation. Thus the central government retains the macro-economic task of reconciling the interests of, say, management and workers; in the short term, wage increases which are claimed in response to price rises and the lifting of subsidies can only be kept within bounds by state intervention. In future, the People's Bank of China will be a crucial instrument in effecting macro-economic adjustments to eliminate the budgetary deficit, curtail the excessive provision of credit and limit inflationary pressures—but without reversing the economic reforms.

The continuing role of central government in macro-economic guidance was highlighted by the priorities of the Seventh Five Year Plan (1986–1990), the final draft of which was presented by Premier Zhao Ziyang to the National People's Congress, China's Parliament, in April 1986. The annual growth targets during the period of the Plan were given as 7.5 percent for industry and 4 percent for agriculture. While the leadership continued to place faith in reform, they were at pains (through the Plan targets) to avoid overheating in terms of excessive industrial construction works and personal consumption. The guiding principles were continuing reform but with lower economic growth; creating a balance between total demand and total supply; improvement of economic efficiency with greater attention to quality control; and finally, stress on material culture but not permitting 'cultural pollution' (that is, Western values overriding the Chinese way of life), or foreign economic domination. As in the Sixth Plan, priorities in the Seventh have been given to agriculture, energy and transportation. Consumer goods like food, some electric appliances, automobiles and motorcycles remain important targets. Significantly, there has been emphasis not so much on the acquisition of plant from abroad as on the renovation and technological restructuring of existing enterprises.

Consequently, investment has been directed towards existing enterprises and tertiary industries like education which serve production. At a Special Communist Party Work Conference in September 1985 calls were made for more foreign technology, equipment and expertise. Decentralisation of decision-making powers to enterprises demands better management skills, and these are best obtained by training abroad or by institutions established by Western educators in China. Education in other fields is equally indispensable for the acquisition of new technical and technological skills as well as the creation of a better educated work-force as a whole. Ultimately, however, technological change as well as better managers and experts will depend on the level of foreign exchange earned by the country's exports.

The prosperity of agriculture was seen as the key to China's economic health. The abolition of the unified grain purchase system in 1985 had been intended to reduce the burden of subsidies on the central treasury but some economic planners were clearly worried by the peasants' lack of enthusiasm for growing grain in the light of the incentives for producing cash crops. In 1985, for example, the grain harvest declined by 7 percent, its first fall for some years, and this was attributed also to peasants taking jobs in rural industry. Self-sufficiency in food is always a sensitive national security issue because of the possibility of war and economic blockade. The Seventh Five Year Plan thus focussed on increasing yields through continuing rural reform and improving agricultural science and technology (subsequently to be applied to grain and other crops). One acknowledged difficulty, however, was that of persuading technical experts to go to the countryside; in China, as in other developing countries, those with high educational qualifications are reluctant to give up the amenities of the cities.

The Plan also called for the construction of key projects in the energy and transportation sectors, without which ambitious programmes in other economic sectors would be held up. The consumption boom meant increased purchases and use of electric appliances in the home and this put further pressure on energy resources already overstrained by accelerated industrial production. China has no lack of energy resources—especially in terms of fossil fuels—but exploitation requires heavy expenditure. In 1985 a Chinese spokesman on energy referred to China's plentiful reserves of coal (estimated at 780 billion tons) and abundant usable water for hydroelectric power generation, but remarked that 60 percent of coal deposits were in the North and 71 percent of hydroelectric resources in the Southwest of China. The bulk of these reserves are thus far from the areas of greater need, the industrial cities of the coast and the Southeast region. In addition, the huge mining centres of the North benefit heavy industry close by and an overburdened transportation system hampers the movement of coal southwards. Ironically, therefore, in spite of China's abundant supplies, coal has often been imported from as far afield as Australia.

Energy policy is bound up with questions of economic strategy.

During the period of the Sixth Five Year Plan (1981–1985), industrial and agricultural production grew more quickly than available energy supplies, and energy conservation measures were undertaken. The Seventh Plan envisages a lower growth rate for high energy-using industries like metallurgy and chemicals relative to that for industry as a whole. In contrast, sectors which consume less energy such as machinery, electronics and home electrical appliances, will have a higher rate of growth. Moreover, local industries—like those newly developed in rural areas—tend to rely on energy sources close at hand, and these will represent a greater share of China's economic output in the years to come. In general, the shift to more high value-added products will contribute to energy conservation.

The findings of oil and gas offshore prospecting have so far been disappointing—though both the Chinese leaders and foreign interests still believe in the potential—and focus in the Seventh Plan is on coal. Some industrial concerns have already shifted from oil to coal. The Plan calls for increased coal production to a billion tons by 1990, an average rate of expansion of 30 to 40 million tons. To achieve this through the large-scale collieries alone would require enormous additional inputs and reduced inputs in other sectors. Some of the growth will be accounted for by opencast mining which needs less funding, and small-scale locally-run pits operating without help from national funds. Development priorities will nevertheless centre on major coal-mining centres like Shanxi Province and the Inner Mongolian Autonomous Region.

While offshore finds of oil have been disappointing, the Chinese leaders attach great importance in the Seventh Five Year Plan to the further development of existing onshore oilfields and the exploration of new sources. A 1990 production goal of 150 million tons has been cited. Priority fields include Daqing and Shengli, the major existing centres, and new sources have been discovered nearby, suggesting Chinese oil reserves in the region of two billion tons. Commercially viable offshore fields are yet to be discovered but prospecting continues.

Coal, however, has remained more important than oil in the thinking of the Chinese leaders and power generation is crucial to development. The Plan called for initial priority to be given to the construction of thermal power stations and the opening of new coal mines for growing energy needs. The exploitation of nuclear and hydroelectric resources required more time and investment and is reserved for the long term. Whether because of environmental considerations or lack of expertise, nuclear power stations are to be constructed only where thermal or hydroelectric supplies are ruled out. While power generation needs, especially in the countryside, are partially being met by small makeshift hydroelectric stations set up by local people, extensive national investment is required if current goals are to be achieved. It is in this field of energy that foreign investment and technology are being sought.[14]

Nowhere is China's inadequate transportation capacity better demonstrated than in the movement of coal; in Shanxi Province, for example, coal was taking up as much as three-quarters of transport capacity in the mid-1980s. Moreover, in the case of other cargo, China's railway system carries an unduly heavy burden. In addition, transport is poorly integrated and co-ordinated, with very little traffic actually using more than one means of carriage. In the past, administration of the transport system has been highly centralised, following the dictates of the command economy, although even prior to the announcement of the Seventh Five Year Plan, greater independence of industrial enterprises (and thus consignors) was leading to demands for greater efficiency. Meanwhile the expanding rural economy and crop diversification have increased the demand for transport services, and local entrepreneurs have been turning to improvised means to fill gaps in transportation capacity.

For transport over long distances, railways will continue to be crucial, and in line with other economic reforms, the first steps were taken in the early 1980s to rationalise and decentralise administration. While there remains a clear-cut division between the national lines built by the State and operated by the Ministry of Railways and local networks constructed and run by provincial authorities, regional branch bureaux of centrally-controlled railways have been reduced in numbers and greater co-ordination between the two systems is being planned. The trend is towards the division of administration and operation, designed to achieve greater co-ordination of services and accountability to users. In accordance with moves in other economic sectors, there have been concessions to local bodies, and possibly such inducements will eventually be extended to private enterprise; thus, local railway administrations have been urged to raise funds themselves (through bank loans, for instance) rather than rely on state subsidies.

Transportation reform in the mid-1980s was still in its infancy but, as one of the priorities of the Seventh Five Year Plan, attention was being paid to the renovation of existing facilities and increasing rail freight capacity. In October 1984 the Ministry called for investment in the railway system by overseas investors; certainly, the transportation sector will be one in which foreign interests will play a major role.

This separation of administration and operation has also been reflected in other sectors like water-borne transportation. In 1984, for example, the Ministry of Communications transferred its control over harbour facilities in the northern port of Tianjin to the city's own Harbour Authority, Shipping Agency, and Foreign Trade Transportation Bureau, all of which are under mainly local jurisdiction.

To date China's road system has been poorly developed and vehicle ownership strictly limited, being mainly confined to public bodies. Private cars are, however, increasing in number, especially among rich entrepreneurs. Increased distribution between the country and the cities has led to an awareness of the need to improve road infrastructure and amenities, and the Seventh Five Year Plan proposes a tax on vehicles to raise revenue for road construction. The central government has kept control, determining major projects and funding the main roads in the light of national needs, but local governments are responsible for local roads, and the trend is towards transferring the responsibility for road maintenance and construction from the Ministry to local bodies. If, however, road transport is to meet the demands placed on it by increased production and more widespread distribution, an injection of foreign technology and capital will be essential not only for the additional infrastructure but also for automobile manufacture, a priority of the Seventh Five Year Plan.

Civil aviation in China is yet to develop its full potential but measures have been taken to separate administration and operation. While the appropriate central body looks after the national interest, in business terms its regional offices are being turned into airline units, each specialising in either domestic or international routes. Subject to independent management, they will be in a position to purchase foreign aircraft, thus offering commercial opportunities to overseas manufacturers.[15]

Against the background of the Seventh Five Year Plan foreign trade is seen by the Chinese leaders as an integral part of their country's economic strategy and will thus play a major part in achieving the goal of quadrupling industrial and agricultural output by the end of the century: it has been estimated that already there are at least twenty million Chinese in employment directly related to exports. The coastal cities are the pace-setters in the expansion of exports necessary to earn the foreign currency to pay for imported capital plant and foreign technology. These centres will play a crucial role in China's economy, processing raw materials into goods for overseas markets. Development of the Southeastern seaboard, however, will bring greater disparities in material wealth between the coast and the hinterland, and this is at variance with the egalitarian social goals of Mao Zedong to which even the current leadership claim to be dedicated in the long term. In addition, the current Chinese leaders have continued to support Third World demands such as better terms of trade for developing countries and are determined to keep their country clear of any suggestion of foreign economic control. They are therefore at pains to emphasise that foreign economic co-operation is clearly defined by China's central government and is justified in ideological terms, as the CCP has to explain every twist and turn of policy in terms of Marxist-Leninist categories. The Party's credibility depends on the correct understanding of the stages of history through which the revolution must pass.

There are post-1949 historical precedents for collaboration with capitalism. When rehabilitating the economy in the 1950s, after decades of foreign invasion and civil war, the Communist leaders utilised the services of capitalists from the old regime and allowed their enterprises to make profits until the so-called socialist transformation had been achieved. Present foreign economic co-operation is similar, even though the Chinese leaders see it as qualitatively different from the situation in the 1950s; joint Sino-foreign enterprises, for example, are designed to earn more foreign currency and acquire management experience, funds and advanced technology from other countries so as to facilitate industrial progress. While the role of such co-operation is supposedly limited to supplementing the socialist economy, it will have far-reaching effects on Chinese society, as institutions are bound to affect values. Most importantly, however, the Chinese gain management experience and skills; the joint enterprises are owned by both the Chinese and foreign investors, with fixed assets belonging to the enterprises as independent juridical persons. Chairmen of boards of directors are appointed by the Chinese partners; the deputy chairmen by foreigners. Control is thus prevented from passing entirely into foreign hands.

Foreign involvement in the Chinese economy nevertheless has its pitfalls for the Chinese. It must first of all be aligned with the country's economic objectives. China's leaders see the first task of foreign trade as promoting the nations's economic development through the expansion of production, increases in domestic trade and promotion of scientific research. But it would be undesirable for foreign investment to be concentrated in certain branches of industry; it makes sense to adopt the erstwhile policy of the Japanese and protect domestic 'infant' industries from excessive foreign investment. Thus technology—which the Chinese wish to buy rather than hardware, often to the resentment of foreign traders—does increase China's industrial potential; extensive outside control of major industries, on the other hand, could stifle China's economic growth in the long run. Thus in poorly developing sectors like television manufacturing, the roles of outside capital and fully foreign-owned companies are prominent and likely to remain so but in those where Chinese technological development is more advanced, like the electrical appliance industry, independent growth has been fostered to satisfy rising domestic demand and with a view to exports. In cases like the latter, too great an inflow of foreign capital would subject the industries to the interests of multi-national parent companies rather than the Chinese leaders' own economic strategy. In addition, to date, foreign investment has often been concentrated in the production of consumer rather than capital goods. Moreover, foreign partners usually wish to sell joint-venture goods in China so that these do not compete with their other products overseas; the Chinese, on the other hand, seek to protect the domestic market and expand exports, thereby avoiding foreign exchange deficits.[16]

Aware of these difficulties and matching official opinion, Chinese trade journal articles have set out major export targets, including increases in sales of manufactured goods abroad (and already these are taking an increasing share of China's exports). Export competitiveness requires more specialist knowledge among managers, both at the macro-economic level of central government and in relation to regular updating in line with world market trends. Issues have encompassed not only technological changes of capital plant but quality control and better international market research. In time the Chinese could equal the Japanese success in selecting export winners through superior design, fashion and quality.

To achieve these goals of greater efficiency and export competitiveness, China's foreign trade bodies are being decentralised as were industrial enterprises. To recapitulate briefly, in the early 1980s the Chinese leaders decided to free enterprises from administrative controls; decision-making was transferred to those actually involved in production, even though the relevant ministries retained responsibility for overall planning and supervision. The Chinese leaders had been promoting changes in the foreign trade system since 1979, but it was only in late 1984 that the State Council, the Chinese equivalent of a Western cabinet, called for thoroughgoing reform. Just as the central government had provided funds for industrial enterprises and distributed their products, so also did it procure exports and allocate imports. As a result, domestic production was divorced from selling abroad and imports were stockpiled and not always put to the best use; in other words there was no accountability about cost, profit and loss. The reforms emphasised the separation of administration and business together with the downward transfer of central government officials. Closer links between industry and trade, technology and trade, and imports and exports were sought through use of the agency system.

Firstly, the Ministry of Foreign Economic Relations and Trade (MOFERT) and foreign trade organs of provincial governments were to confine their activities to administration and not directly participate in trade. Trading companies themselves were to have greater initiative in management matters, being responsible for their own profit and loss. MOFERT was nevertheless in overall control, providing the conditions and guide-lines within which trade bodies were to operate. MOFERT retained the authority to formulate policy in terms of national priorities and oversee its implementation; it was to prepare long-term trade development programmes in co-operation with the State Planning Commission. It would have the task of balancing imports and exports and of determining policy towards individual countries through government-by-government negotiations regarding international trade and commercial representation. Approval of important technical transfers and brand names as well as surveys of world markets also fell within MOFERT's jurisdiction. It was also to be responsible for reporting appointments of members of trading company committees to local authorities. At the national level it has been given the function of promoting training in foreign economic relations. Within this chain of command, provincial committees in charge of foreign trade were responsible for supervising local trading companies. In order to further the managerial

independence of trading companies, national export procurement plans were abolished except for some essential commodities
and those involved in agreements between governments. Most
goods had previously been under the control of the major national trade corporations which, even after the reform, continued
to supervise their local branches.

The aims of the reforms were embodied in the evolution of
the old and the creation of new trade organisations. The National
Trade Corporations were to continue to monopolise dealings in
certain essential items. To promote export expansion, local trading corporations have been created since 1980, the Shanghai
Foreign Trade Corporation being a case in point. In addition,
there are now trading companies affiliated with the national industrial sector and established by central government bodies in
charge of manufacturing; included in this category is the China
National Machinery and Equipment Export Corporation set up
by the Ministry of Machine Building Industry. Moreover, some
bodies like certain steel corporations are now allowed to conduct
export business on their own. Likewise specialised export groups
can be formed by a number of factories in the same line of
production, taking joint responsibility for profit and loss. Especially in order to secure the link between production and business,
joint trading ventures have been initiated between industrial and
trading companies. Finally, a few specialist bodies like the China
Silk Corporation engage in production and also sell on the domestic as well as the export market.

These reforms of foreign trade institutions have been designed
to increase productivity and ensure greater accountability. By
the mid-1980s the Chinese leaders were also experimenting with
new arrangements but with the same objective of increasing incentives and profits: one was the Export-Import Agency Business
whereby a trading company exports and imports on a consign-
ment basis and receives a commission, the manufacturers and
users rather than the central government taking the risk. Separate import and export agencies have been established on similar
principles.[17]

In the long term these reforms will contribute to China's economic growth, and trends to date have been encouraging. Yet
liberalising the foreign trade system—by giving greater initiative
to a variety of trading companies and granting greater financial
independence to local bodies—has not been problem-free. Chinese Communist officials, both central and local, have been
trained in the practices and procedures of a command economy

and are consequently ill-equipped to handle the sophisticated mechanisms of a more flexible trade system. In a command economy privilege extends to officials by virtue of position rather than personal attainment; in many cases they clearly resent the financial clout of managers in the trading companies whom they see as a threat to their own vested interests. There is also insufficient administrative expertise in Chinese officialdom to do justice to the new economic institutions. By 1985 there was glaring abuse of the foreign trade system for personal gain and against the national interest, particularly in the field of imports; local trade companies had imported too many consumer goods like home electrical appliances and too little foreign technology for the expansion of exports. Perhaps the most notorious case of corruption was the Hainan scandal of 1985 as a result of which a number of Communist Party and government officals were dismissed. Hainan—a subtropical island off the Southern coast of Guangdong Province—had earlier been designated an 'open port', with special powers to import goods and retain foreign exchange. Permitted imports of vehicles and other luxury goods were originally intended for infrastructural development and use on Hainan only. Entrepreneurs in government departments and even schools claimed that they required vehicles and other items for their official duties, and with bank loans in Chinese currency, they acquired US $570 million worth of foreign exchange to pay for the goods from abroad. Many of these were then illegally sold to consumers in other provinces and at a huge profit. The scandal, involving 88 government departments in Hainan, pointed to the fragility of the new economic institutions. Moreover, for their part in approving the transactions in Hainan, local officials received illegal bonuses and then decided to start trading themselves, encouraging administrative units to set up companies and thereby disregarding central government regulations which prohibited officials from commercial trading. Hainan was only the tip of the iceberg; there were other cases where officials with the power to approve the use of foreign currencies or issue import and export licenses had accepted concurrent appointments as officers of trade corporations.[18]

By mid-1985 the central government was taking corrective measures, though these signalled an adjustment rather than a reversal of foreign trade reform; these included levying import-adjustment taxes over and above existing tariffs and tightening the surveillance of foreign currency use as well as the 'extra-mural' activities of local officials. Many problems had undoubtedly sprung from the rapid proliferation of foreign trade companies, and in April 1985 MOFERT announced new rules for their establishment. In addition, the initiative of local trading companies was further restricted by a new system of licenses imposed on a wide range of exports. Taxes were also put on certain export items.

Legislation, however, can only go so far in remedying abuses even if greater financial controls by the banking system can reduce the misuse of funds. The removal of Jin Deqin as President of the Bank of China and his replacement by Madame Chen Muhua, formerly Minister of Foreign Trade, was attributed in part to the sudden decline of China's foreign exchange reserves. Clearly, until the new foreign trade bodies and financial mechanisms are well established, the application of central government measures will depend on the integrity, personal qualities and adaptability of managers of trading companies and officials in local administration.

Only if the Chinese set up a good track record for reliability will they be able to encourage investment from abroad in ventures up in the Special Economic Zones on China's coast. It is through the experience of the zones designated in the early 1980s—as well as other 'open cities' granted separate status in 1984—that Sino-foreign economic co-operation will be examined. Before doing this, however, brief reference will be made to Chinese leaders' industrial strategy and the infusion of technology from overseas. Because of their material wealth and technical skills, major cultural and scientific centres like Shanghai and Guangzhou (Canton) have been chosen as Economic Development Zones into which new technologies will be imported and put to use for later transference to other parts of China. As a result of foreign technology, new industries will be created and existing ones transformed. China's Seventh Five Year Plan has given priority to the improvement of traditional industries; these are labour-intensive, and include sectors like machinery, metallurgy and automobiles as well as electric power and transport. Developed countries are moving out of heavy industrial sectors, and in the long term the Chinese will also turn to the new technologies after current goals like the creation of better infrastructure and the improvement of existing plant have been achieved. Ultimately the Chinese will innovate and create their own advanced technologies but meanwhile they will rely on imported knowledge in areas such as computers (for automation), optical fibre communications and biological engineering. Chinese research is already under way and this calls for the development of 'silicon glens' and 'scientific gardens' where enterprises can integrate research, production and information. Foreign technology input is intended to improve China's ability to produce goods formerly imported. Economic Development Zones are designed as domestic vantage points from which to observe world scientific, technical and economic trends as well as to train managers and other specialists.[19]

The Special Economic Zones (SEZs) were seen as pioneers in these matters even if they were not initially as successful as the Chinese leaders had hoped. Perhaps the most famous of the zones is Shenzhen, and like the others, was set up to attract foreign investment, patents and technology. To get personnel in fields like science, technology and management, graduates trained overseas are being sought not only for their specialised knowledge but also for their independence of mind, a quality indispensable for the creativity and innovation required of China's modernisation programme.

On the face of it, zones like Shenzhen have certain advantages from the point of view of rapid economic development. Virtually a 'greenfield' site in the early 1980s, Shenzhen itself has a new infrastructure from which modern facilities can benefit. But the performance of the zones has been disappointing to the Chinese authorities; originally conceived as being industry-orientated and geared to the export of manufactured goods, by the mid-1980s they were heavily dependent on Chinese domestic sales for their economic expansion. Because Shenzhen did not then impose tariffs, it could charge lower prices and thereby attract customers from the Chinese hinterland and Hong Kong, turning itself into a retail trade centre. In addition, resources were focussed on tourism and the provision of amenities rather than manufacturing capacity, and the manufacturing that did exist used low rather than high technology. Shenzhen was also relying to a large extent on the central government for construction funds. Consequently, the main purposes of zones like Shenzhen were not being fulfilled; they had been designed to generate foreign currency earnings, and to encourage imputs of foreign technology, not produce consumer goods for the domestic market. Moreover, the zones were meant to procure their development funds from foreign investors, given the special powers they enjoyed in that respect. Solutions to these problems may be only a matter of time. In view of the Seventh Five Year Plan general overheating of the economy, called for a curb on investment for the first two years, and this could also prove an incentive for the Zone authorities to find more foreign sources of capital. In any case, as the industrial base (say, in Shenzhen) matures and manufacturing processes and product quality improve, the Zone's goods will be able to compete more effectively on world markets.

Though often cautiously optimistic, foreign investors have from the outset been aware of the risk element. Priority in the Seventh Five Year Plan is given to transport and energy, investment in which involves long lead-times and slow returns for investors. Thus will thermal power plants, built through joint ventures with foreign concerns, become profitable enough for overseas investors before the expiry of the term of the project? Moreover, an increase in joint ventures could result in shortages of raw materials which foreign investors have tended not to take into account. There may well be pressures too on the availability of skilled manpower. Nevertheless, with these caveats, the future of the Special Economic Zones and joint ventures looks bright and they seem set to make a major contribution to China's modernisation programme. In the 1980s the Chinese authorities were already taking steps to assure foreign investors of China's goodwill; for instance, royalties in connection with advanced technological knowhow are not liable to tax, and tax concessions have been operative on the importation of plant and equipment essential to new ventures in collaboration with foreign concerns. Investment protection treaties were signed in the mid-1980s with France, Belgium and the Federal Republic of Germany.

Just as granting autonomy to industrial enterprises and foreign trade organs reflected the need to make China's economy more receptive to overseas trade and investment, likewise were the reforms of the education system in the mid-1980s intended to train the new kinds of qualified manpower required by the country's modernisation programme. The Seventh Five Year Plan (1986-1990) called for priority to be given to training scientists, technologists and managerial personnel, both for industry and agriculture—needs to be satisfied partly by graduates from China's universities and additionally by Chinese students educated abroad. Traditionally, and even up to the late 1970s, China could hardly have been considered a 'pluralist' society; there was only one source of political authority. Officially, the position of the Communist Party remains unquestioned but there are embryos of new independent centres of economic power. In advanced Western industrial societies the professions have long occupied an honoured place; in China they are just coming into their own. Autonomy of industrial concerns and tentative moves towards private enterprise have made contractual obligations more complex and demands have grown for adjudication and arbitration procedures within both the public and private sectors. China needs not only scientists, technologists and industrial managers but lawyers and accountants as well.

China must train a whole range of experts to deal with the increasingly complex nature of an advanced industrial society. Until the late 1970s factory directors and lower-level managers were appointed on the basis of political criteria, and secretaries of Communist Party committees had the major say in decision-making. The new industrial policy, however, places a premium on initiative and innovation, and the country is desperately short of middle management capable of effective leadership. Accordingly, in the mid- 1980s, universities and enterprises were being called upon to increase the number of management institutes and courses. At that time existing institutes were producing more than 5,000 managers and executives each year, but quality and quantity were still below par. Specialisms being taught ranged from the use of computers to international monetary affairs, economics and labour laws, and institutes have since helped enterprises to plan their own management training classes with a view to retaining older personnel. In addition, new training programmes for rural leaders were being instituted throughout China to teach agro-technical and management skills.[20]

Professional needs also governed university enrolment priorities, and in 1985 there was a sharp increase in the numbers enrolled for finance and law courses as well as management. In the same year the first special class of business law graduates, originally recruited from various ministries and judicial bodies, completed their studies at two major universities. In 1984 it had been announced that there were 18,500 lawyers in China, a number of whom were engaged as legal advisers to government agencies and enterprises. In 1985 in the wake of China's open-door policy, economic reforms at home and increased private ownership of the means of production, legislation on accountancy law was passed. It is in these service sectors as well as in finance and banking that foreign enterprise could, and indeed already has, played a role in training personnel.

The key to expanding the management, legal and financial service sectors lies in an attitude of mind cultivated over decades since the beginning of the industrial revolution in Western Europe. In China obedience to one source of political authority has persisted until the present day and is only slowly giving way to the acceptance of an entrepreneurial spirit, the hallmark of capitalism along with its legal and financial institutions. It is the task of the education system to foster creativity through independent thought and opinion and to get away from the rote learning and conformity of past curricula: to this end the humanities and social sciences are as important as science and technology. Moreover, fostering individual aptitudes and a humanistic outlook is itself to be commended.

During the mid-1980s institutional reforms in education were intended to achieve these objectives and, like changes in the industrial sector, designed to encourage individual initiative; the logic of market forces was applied wherever possible. The autonomy of institutions, particularly universities, was seen as necessary to achieve the specialist manpower needs of China's modernisation programme. At the top of the system stands the State Education Commission, established in 1985, and replacing the old Ministry of Education; this is responsible for national policy-making and overall development planning. Education is seen as an utilitarian matter; breadth of learning is sacrificed in favour of practical knowledge and equality of opportunity subordinated to the demands of a developing economy. In discussing the Seventh Five Year Plan (1986–1990), the Communist Party Central Committee stated the priority of producing many more graduates in science, technology and management, and at the same time called for a strengthening of educational links with industry. In addition to devolving responsibility on to university presidents and heads of secondary and primary schools—with party committees relegated to an advisory role—the state has given institutional leaders (especially in the tertiary sector) greater control over their finances in the hope of improving efficiency, preventing wastage and ensuring greater accountability. Thus, while as before 1985, the state continues to fund higher education, universities are expected to seek other sources of finance, and even to make a profit through collaboration with industry. As in the case of industrial enterprises, the new freedoms granted to educational institutions extend to hiring and firing personnel, with academic tenure being abolished. In addition, staff may select their own research projects and engage in commercially profitable ventures on an institutional, departmental or individual basis. If senior officals in higher education are insufficiently entrepreneurial, academic staff may press for their dismissal.

The same kind of principle is being applied to the university enrolment process which, although still directed by central government bodies, has been made flexible enough to take account of the new closer links between education and industry. Thus since 1985 institutions have enjoyed greater discretionary powers in enrolling students, especially from industry. This linkage between the economy and the universities is reinforced by greater flexibility in the allocation of graduates, and whereas previously the state often sent the latter to jobs inappropriate to their qualifications, students' study is now more closely tied to their future careers. Moreover, like academic staff pay, the financial support of students is linked to performance; higher education is no longer free and scholarships are only awarded on merit, the best students being sponsored by the state, employers or institutions. Grants are provided for those in financial difficulties and for special categories of students like those undergoing teacher training, particularly those in technical subjects. Secondary vocational schools and basic skills at the primary level are being awarded priority. If academically acceptable, students not in receipt of scholarships or financial assistance are permitted to enrol if they pay their own fees.

Nevertheless, in spite of the prerogatives given to institutions, the state retains the final responsibility for the assessment of performance. Successful institutions will be rewarded but the inefficient restructured or closed down, the emphasis being on lucrative and economically relevant research projects as well as up-to-date courses and curricula which teachers have the freedom to devise according to student needs.

On the face of it the educational reforms will produce a system that is market-orientated, elitist in its selection of the best students and rather narrowly focussed on science and technology. Yet educational policy in the mid-1980s did suggest a concerted attempt to create a better educated work-force, and at a time when only 4 percent of Chinese Communist Party members had received a university education. Primary education is almost universal even though in rural areas it often means only four years of study as opposed to six in the cities. In May 1985 a national educational conference stated that the institution of a nine-year compulsory education system was a major target.[21]

These economic and educational reforms are crucial if China is to absorb foreign investment and technology; on their successful implementation rests the credibility of the Chinese leaders at home and abroad, and in turn, their modernisation programme. The contribution of the EC countries to this endeavour is dealt with in the next chapter.

3
China-EC Trade and Economic Co-operation

As the might of Western power impinged on declining Chinese dynastic power in the mid-nineteenth century, European traders saw China as a vast market waiting to be tapped; similarly, their counterparts today believe that China's economic growth will offer them great export potential, and they take comfort from the outward-looking policies of Deng Xiaoping. Moreover, the CCP leaders, mindful of their unfortunate experience in the 1950s when the Russians attempted to bring China under Soviet domination, wish to maintain their country's independence by diversifying markets and sources of supply to avoid undue reliance on the USA, for example. The EC also faces competition in the China market from Japan which, by virtue of geographical proximity, a common cultural heritage and economic complementarity, is already a formidable rival to the Community. But, in view of Chinese charges in 1985 and 1986 that the Japanese had sold obsolete machinery to China and been reluctant to transfer the latest technology lest it facilitate competition against Japan on world markets, it is clear that the Japanese will not be permitted to become dominant in all of China's economic sectors. Consequently, in recent years the Chinese leaders have taken initiatives to strengthen ties with the EC, as shown by frequent visits of Chinese leaders to EC countries. In July 1986, for instance, Li Peng, China's Deputy Premier, emphasised economic and technical ties between China and the EC in a meeting with Jacques Delors, President of the EC Commission. These ties were in three main areas: importing more Chinese goods, providing loans to China on favourable terms, and setting up enterprises in China run jointly with or entirely by foreigners.

This theme of independence and spheres of co-operation must be seen within the broader framework of China's long-term modernisation programme as well as the more immediate perspective of the Seventh Five Year Plan (1986–1990). On a visit to Britain in July 1985, Premier Zhao Ziyang spoke of his country's modernisation in terms of two stages: in the first, from 1980 to the turn of the century, gross industrial and agricultural output will be quadrupled, with a moderately high standard of living attained; in the second, the first fifty years of the twenty-first century, China will reach the level of the world's developed countries. Economic reforms are being pioneered in the rural areas and then introduced to the cities; in their greater exposure to the outside world the coastal areas are pace-setters for the hinterland.

The Seventh Five Year Plan set down the major priorities of energy, transport, communications, raw materials industries, and machinery and electronics, and it is in these sectors that the Chinese are seeking European technology and co-operation. Shortages of electric power have hampered industrial and general economic growth, and the exploitation of China's abundant coal and hydroelectric power is a target area for foreign investment. Coal provided 79 percent of the country's total energy requirements in 1983, and foreign expertise is invited to renovate and expand existing mines as well as develop new ones. Offshore oil prospecting, where foreign participation has been concentrated in the early and middle 1980s, has so far proved disappointing. Because of this and in order to revive flagging western enthusiasm, in 1985 the China National Offshore Oil Corporation (CNOOC) reduced the fees charged to successful foreign bidders for prospecting rights and at the same time gave other concessions to further develop the smaller fields already discovered.

Inadequate transportation has been a constraint on increasing energy supply and particular importance is attached to extending the railway system. In addition, with the greater mobility of people, goods and services, roads (particularly between major cities) as well as port facilities need to be extended and upgraded. An increasingly complex modern economy will also offer scope for Sino-European co-operation in the telecommunications sector, promising lucrative opportunities for Western companies.

Likewise the remaining priority, the development of raw materials along with the metallurgical, chemical and construction industries, has been held back by China's outmoded infrastructure and lack of up-to-date expertise; the mining and processing of mineral resources required the latest Western technology.

Finally, upgrading the production facilities in the machinery and electronics industries is crucial for diversifying China's exports of manufactured goods.

Thus the Seventh Five Year Plan envisages an important role

for foreign trade in China's development strategy. In the past the Chinese have been reluctant to incur heavy overseas debts, and in the mid-1980s annual debt repayments only accounted for a small percentage of China's foreign earnings, much less than the accepted safe ratio of 20 percent. The keynote is still self-reliance, foreign aid being strictly complementary. Nevertheless senior officials announced, in early 1986, that they would increase foreign borrowing, including government and commercial loans—even though state control over debt was to be strengthened—with the Bank of China in charge of foreign exchange. But clearly much would continue to depend on the imports of capital plant and technology. Annual average increases in value of 8 percent for exports and 6 percent for imports were projected for the period of the Plan, the leadership being mindful of the 1985 foreign trade deficit.[1]

The export drive is being promoted on three levels. Firstly, the freer play of market forces is intended to improve the standard and effectiveness of export goods, and an added incentive in this direction was the institution of an official system to reward excellence and certify products, with a network of official inspectors appointed on a regional and industrial enterprise basis.[2] A second approach was to speed up the trend in export commodity structure away from primary products towards certain types of high technology value-added goods, especially as China's labour cost advantages *vis à vis* other developing countries in sectors like textiles are likely to decrease over time; and in any case China's goods may face growing protectionism in EC markets. The third approach was to establish up-to-date plant for manufacturing export goods in the coastal areas, particularly in the Special Economic Zones.

The Plan's import strategy was two-fold. First of all, emphasis was put on importing capital plant, advanced technology, computer software, and urgently needed raw materials, with the renovation of industrial plant in North-east China being a priority objective. The purchase of foreign consumer goods as well as production lines for these was strictly controlled, and simultaneously in 1986 more important goods were made subject to licensing. Imports, however, will remain closely tied to export levels, and the Chinese leaders are attracted to 'compensation' trade, a system whereby a foreign partner providing capital, technology and facilities is repaid through the goods produced. In this scenario both sides have an interest in maintaining good faith: foreign suppliers will only receive high quality goods if they furnish the best technology; the Chinese side, which obtains ownership of the plant on conclusion of the contract, is only likely to acquire further technology in similar deals in the future if the resulting products are up to international standards. There is every incentive for the Chinese to upgrade the skills of their work-force.

Imports, then, are directed towards modernisation goals rather than to satisfy the growing desire for foreign luxury goods, and even the purchase of large-scale capital plant has become more selective. Nevertheless, as the Chinese peasantry has been encouraged to diversify their production towards cash crops for export, essential items such as grain and cotton may well have to be imported in the long term. Given the domestic demand for consumer goods—encouraged by the Chinese leaders as an incentive for the work-force—as well as the development internationally of the ever-more advanced technologies China needs, imports are bound to increase. In dealing with this issue, Chinese economic journals in the mid-1980s were discussing the case for policies of import substitution.[3]

Import substitution means that certain manufactured goods— the demand for which cannot be satisfied domestically—are initially imported, but later the relevant technology is adopted so that the complete production process may be undertaken in China itself. This strategy comes close to the post-war Japanese policy of the 1950s of acquiring technology from abroad by license rather than spending funds on research in Japan. By the early 1980s the Japanese had become world leaders in certain research fields but the earlier Japanese-type policy is proving attractive to Chinese leaders, as it saves time and cost. Through technology imports, Japan achieved in fifteen years what had taken Europe and the United States half a century. Between 1950 and 1970 Japan spent US $6 billion on buying and assimilating technology while the original research and invention of these patents abroad cost thirty or forty times as much. The Japanese placed more emphasis on importing soft items, that is to say, the rights to use patents, blueprints, technical knowhow and other pure technology—than on hard items like advanced equipment even though their purchase was crucial for the policy of 'reverse engineering'. This calls for a systematic in-depth analysis of as wide a variety of the same kinds of foreign products as possible, with a view to design improvement and further innovation. Because China's basic research effort so far has been directed primarily towards application and development, and given Premier Zhao Ziyang's statement that half of the projected fourfold increase in agricultural and industrial production will be achieved by the input of new scientific and technological knowledge, policies of import substitution and reverse engineering seem well suited to China's needs. In summary, the Chinese leaders' long-term objective is to absorb and adapt technology in these ways; initially concentrating on the coastal cities, the technology will then be transferred to the hinterland where eventually high-value added goods will be produced for both domestic use and export.

This strategy presupposes a Western willingness to transfer advanced technology but, in view of their resentment concerning what they allege is Japan's reluctance to offer direct technological investment, China's leaders are now more inclined to turn to EC countries like West Germany. In addition, the Chinese could well restrict computer imports unless they are accompanied by technology transfer. In the long term the Chinese may choose to protect native 'infant' industries (say, in electronics and computers as well as indigenous technology) by controlling the import of both foreign goods and software, as the Japanese often have. Thus certain features of Japan's experience remain pertinent to China's future development.

One feature of Japan's post-war economic success has been the close relationship between business and government which has helped in the selection of product winners for world markets, and there is surely a lesson here for China. While the recent economic reforms have allowed more initiative to industrial management, and the newly created import and export companies made foreign trade more flexible and efficient in operation, there is more need than ever for overall state guidance in the sphere of technology imports. Take, for example, Japan's 'administrative guidance' system whereby MITI consulted technical specialists to determine the orientation and emphasis of technological development. In this connection, aware of the need to avoid any duplication of technology imports, China's central government in 1985 issued regulations concerning the examination and approval of technology import contracts. Another aspect of Japan's experience, said by Chinese experts to be worth copying, is the payment of subsidies to enterprises importing the most advanced technology.[4]

Nevertheless, however much the Chinese leaders may seek to emulate Japan's approach to technology imports, they are reluctant to rely too heavily on the Japanese connection. By the mid-1980s an integral part of their development strategy was to quadruple import and export volume by the turn of the century, the main focus being closer relations with the EC (even though trade expansion with Western Europe pre-dated the open-door policy launched in the late 1970s). With the onset of the Sino-Soviet dispute China's trade with the Eastern bloc fell while that with the non-Communist world rose.

West German exports to China, for example, tripled in 1958. In line with their new diplomacy, however, the Chinese have not ruled out trade and economic co-operation with the Soviet Union, especially since much of their industrial plant was originally built in the 1950s with Russian assistance. In July 1985 the two countries signed a long-term trade and economic agreement by which the Soviet Union contracted to help modernise factories—for instance, in the North-eastern province of Heilongjiang, a linen factory, a paper mill and an industrial alcohol plant. This is paid for in Chinese goods and foodstuffs, as all Sino-Soviet trade is barter in order not to use precious foreign currency. Soviet exports include steel, non-ferrous metals, lumber, cement and chemical industrial products. The Soviet market is also advantageous from China's point of view, having considerable growth potential, since Western demand for Chinese exports like cotton and textile goods is unlikely to grow rapidly in the present international climate. Moreover, given China's poor rail transport system and need for port expansion, exports and imports from the hinterland are subject to delays; thus cross-border trade with the Soviet Union sometimes appears a better proposition. Statistics for the mid-1980s indicate a continuing upward trend in Sino-Soviet trade, with Russia accounting for 2.4 percent of China's total imports and exports in 1984, a quarter of the ten-nation EC share.[5] But while this limited, though rising, stake in the Chinese economy is partly intended to balance any undue Western influence, China's factory directors are the first to admit that Soviet machinery will have to be made up by more advanced equipment from the West, and the Chinese still have reservations about the quality of Soviet products in general.

Experience and closer economic contact with the West in recent years have made the Chinese much more discerning in their purchase of foreign goods and technology. Surveys of China's post-war relations with individual countries—like the Federal Republic of Germany, Great Britain and France—published in Chinese journals stress the individual technological strengths of different countries and point to the diversity of skills and resources in the EC as a whole. Moreover, the Community, with its high standard of living and sophisticated consumer demand, is a great potential market for China's exports. Diplomatic relations at Community level were established with China in 1975, and total two-way trade doubled between that year and 1979. Although growth slowed down in 1980 as a result of China's economic readjustment policy, the general trend is upward; trade between China and the Common Market was worth US $5.6 billion in 1984 compared with $1.6 billion in 1975. In 1984 China had an adverse balance with the EC and trade was clearly more crucial to the former than the latter. In 1984 China's exports to the EC were 8.8 percent of China's world total and her imports from the EC equal to 13.4 percent of her total purchases from abroad; at the same time, Chinese exports in 1984 were a mere 0.4 percent of EC imports, and China was only twenty-eighth in order among the Community's importing trade partners.

Nevertheless, in the mid-1980s, the EC was an important market for China's traditional exports. Raw materials like cotton, raw silk and leather have continued to be sold to the Community's processing industries as have various kinds of non-ferrous metals and ores like copper, lead, tin, manganese and aluminum. In terms of agricultural and associated products, individual EC countries continue to provide stable markets for tea, pig bristles and canned goods. As discussed earlier on, however, export drives have often been cramped by poor quality control on the part of the Chinese, as in the case of textiles which are also vulnerable to protectionist calls. On the other hand demand for China's unique and specialist handicraft goods is likely to rise along with new and more sophisticated consumer tastes. In addition, as manufactured goods increase as a proportion of China's exports, there is scope for diversification into sectors such as machine tools and metalworking machinery which the EC both imports and exports. In recent years much reference has been made to horizontal trade whereby each country specialises within a particular kind of manufacturing, thereby avoiding trade friction. This is particularly relevant to Japan's trade relations with Europe but as China's long-term modernisation goals are achieved, the time may not be far off when Chinese goods become competitive with European products. In the mid-1980s, there were EC complaints against Chinese imports, mainly about low prices and excessive quantities of goods like bristle brushes, though these have been minor in comparison to anti-Japanese strictures. In fact, trade developments have been monitored in accordance with agreements between China and the Community, the first of which was concluded in April 1978. Tariffs have been governed by 'most favoured nation' treatment, with the aim of moving towards a trade balance between both sides. The Chinese agreed to give consideration to more imports from the Community while the latter promised gradually to liberalise the entry of Chinese goods, a joint committee meeting being held annually to achieve these objectives.

China's economic health will increasingly depend on her exports to pay for imports which relate to the priorities of her development programme—steel products, chemical fertilisers and machinery being among the traditional items supplied by the EC countries to China.[6]

Trade between China and her largest EC trading partner, West Germany, was worth US $2.2 billion in 1984, an eightfold increase over 1972 when post-war diplomatic relations were established between the two countries. Surveying the progress of Sino-German exports and imports since 1972, Chinese press articles have pointed out trends similar to those in China's trade with the Community as a whole. While during the early and middle 1980s there were substantial increases in Chinese imports of capital goods—machinery for textiles, treating leather and processing food as well as pumps and compressed air machines for modernisation purposes—deliveries of raw materials, semi-finished goods and primary products grew more slowly. An indication of West German predominance in certain industrial sectors was that, during the period of her Sixth Five Year Plan (1981–1985), of the 6,000 or so items of design and manufacturing technology introduced by China, West Germany accounted for a 30 percent share compared with the US 20 percent and Japan's 15 percent. This pre-eminence also appeared in the value of the Federal Republic's industrial plant exports to China during 1978–84, the figure being $2,463 million compared with $855 million for Britain, $828 million for the USA and $684 million for France.[7] There were even more dramatic changes in China's exports; whereas in 1972 about 70 percent of China's exports to the Federal Republic were native and livestock products, by 1983 their share had dropped to 25 percent; the proportion of manufactured goods increased substantially, chemical products being China's largest single export to West Germany in 1983.[8] In accordance with their social practice, the Chinese are concerned to develop personal relationships with foreign traders, and the importance of the German connection goes back to the

1920s and 1930s, and no doubt post-war German businessmen have been given advice concerning the vicissitudes of the China market from their pre-war counterparts.

The British, like the Germans and other major European powers, were active in pre-war trade with China: the '48 Group of Companies' who built on previous links and pioneered Chinese trade amid adverse post-war political conditions, is highly esteemed by the Chinese. The signing of the Joint Declaration on Hong Kong in 1984 has been cited by both the British and the Chinese as a firm basis for future trade and economic cooperation. During a visit to Britain by Premier Zhao Ziyang in 1985 both sides contracted to provide favourable conditions for trade under the terms of an agreement to run from January 1986 to December 1990. A month earlier a financial agreement had been signed whereby a dual sterling/dollar currency deposit facility was made available. Under this agreement British banks could make funds available to the Bank of China through the Export Credits Guarantee Department, a means of giving credit in an acceptable form to China, a country whose leaders have often appeared reluctant to accept loans, especially from commercial sources. British industrialists had previously complained of being at a disadvantage *vis-à-vis* their European competitors who were benefiting from similar arrangements provided by their own governments. It remains to be seen, however, whether what are in effect government subsidies will be effective in coping with the challenges presented by, say, cheap Japanese finance, but these measures have nevertheless pointed to the importance of the Chinese market to the British economy.

In the mid-1980s, Britain was still one of China's major trading partners: in 1984, for instance, China imported $790 million worth of goods from Britain while her exports were worth $450 million, and the balance remained in Britain's favour in 1985. China's imports from the United Kingdom followed the general EC pattern and included steel, chemical fibres, precision instruments, copper and technical equipment. Prominent among China's exports were cotton, tea, bristles, other agricultural products and textiles.[9] In the mid-1980s British officials and industrialists had good reason to be optimistic about the growth of trade with China, as Britain's expertise in sectors like telecommunications, transportation and energy fitted the priorities of China's economic strategy. There is continuing demand—especially in the advanced coastal provinces of China—for more extensive communications systems, and in 1985 a new telephone link across

Guangdong Province was inaugurated by Cable and Wireless. The company was not new to China, having first operated in Asia in the 1870s, but it began to develop post-war contacts with the Communist regime in the early 1970s from its Hong Kong base, at a time when only six telephone lines linked the mainland with the colony. This was later increased and by 1985, 3,000 lines had been installed to connect twenty-five provincial towns from Fujian Province via Guangzhou to Hainan Island. The huge business potential which China offers, however, is inhibited by the small number of subscribers—mostly senior officals and party and state bodies, the majority of other telephones being in offices or public buildings. But with the encouragement of private business and increased foreign business contacts, this pattern will change. A draft of the Seventh Five Year Plan spoke of allocating a lot of resources to telecommunications; it was projected that the number of telephones, five million in 1985, would treble by 1990 and reach 33 million by the turn of the century.[10]

China's economic reforms have also opened up opportunities for British industry in the transportation sector; witness a contract signed by Short Brothers, the Belfast aircraft manufacturers, to deliver eight 36-seat commuter planes to China's state airline, CAAC, in 1985. With increasing population mobility and numbers of foreign tourists, domestic air services are being upgraded under the jurisdiction of provincial authorities which are free to set up their own autonomous regional airlines and negotiate purchases with foreign suppliers.[11]

The Chinese have shown a clear preference for British suppliers in connection with energy projects, including a major coal-fired power station on the Yangtse River for which both General Electric and Northern Electrical Industries were bidding in 1985. Although defence is not the top priority of the modernisation programme, China is a huge potential arms market and this brings into question the restrictions on the sale of high technology to China. In 1985 British military equipment exports to China were only worth £30 million, small in comparison to major suppliers like Israel. Inhibiting factors in this field have been the decision of COCOM, the Paris-based co-ordinating committee which performs the role of limiting strategic exports to Communist countries liable to threaten Western security. In late 1985, however, the committee removed some items from the restricted list, a decision which—even though relating mainly to high technology products like computers rather than military hardware—

would cut out the lengthy process of approval, thus offering greater scope for arms exporters. While these rules applied equally to the USA, the NATO allies and Japan, the British have often been at a further disadvantage in that their companies do not always receive the support which other European competitors receive from their governments, that is to say, the full backing of senior serving officers in military sales teams.

In other fields, too, the British face competition, partly because of generous assistance given by other EC governments, the food trade being a case in point. With a higher standard of living, particularly in the coastal cities, have come dietary change and demands for more choice in food and drink. British industrialists in these sectors are aiming to double their trade with China during the period of the Seventh Five Year Plan, as the Chinese acknowledge Britain's leading position in food technology and envisage a major British contribution to the modernisation of China's food processing industries.

Interest-free loans and export credits offered by the Danish government to China in the early 1980s have stimulated bilateral trade, especially in financing purchases of dairy products, refined sugar and other comestibles. The importation of refrigeration equipment points to a growing Danish role in China's food processing industries. These products, together with chemical fertilisers and electronic equipment, make up China's main imports from Denmark. In exchange, textiles, handicrafts, canned foods and other light industrial goods are China's important exports to Denmark.

Given the commitment to an ambitious modernisation programme, China's economic 'open-door' policy will not be reversed since an expansion of exports is necessary to pay for imported technology and capital.

Increasing Chinese stress on the export of high value-added products, already aimed at design and fashion-conscious Western markets, indicates that in the long term a greater proportion of Chinese exports will be destined for the developed economies of the EC, North America and Japan, always providing that Chinese quality-control problems can be overcome and production diversified. These trends offer scope for further Sino-European economic co-operation, especially joint ventures.

Fears lest undesirable aspects of Western culture and foreign economic domination go along with co-operation and investment from abroad have prompted a spate of articles justifying and defining the scope of joint ventures. In the early 1950s, in order to promote the rehabilitation of a war-torn economy and lay the groundwork for the transition of socialism, CCP leaders in augurated a period of New Democracy, a programme during which capitalist enterprises were not taken over by the state but their owners—erstwhile supporters of the previous régime—were enlisted in support of short-term economic objectives. Eventually, major industrial sectors were to come under state control but the reforms of the 1980s have turned back the clock, decentralising decision-making power and encouraging the operation of market forces, albeit within the framework of the command economy. Moreover, current policy on foreign economic co-operation has carried the New Democracy one stage further, and a recent CCP source spoke of the 'open-door' policy being necessary even when the final stage of Communism has been reached. Some Chinese ideological purists, however, will have argued that means determine ends and that capitalist values will subvert final Communist goals. In other words, will it in the long term be possible to eradicate capitalist values, the existence of which is an unavoidable result of a foreign economic presence? In response, CCP spokesmen, while conceding the danger of the spread of bourgeois ideology, have pointed out the advantages of scientific and technological exchanges and that coexistence with foreign capitalism takes place under Chinese state laws and planning.

There are various other ways in which the efficiency of Chinese industry may be enhanced and its interests protected. Joint ventures are said to confer advantages on both partners. Foreign investors, in directly participating in management and taking risks, will want the enterprise to be profitable, and thus they have every incentive to put their skills at the disposal of their Chinese partners, usually a state enterprise. From the Chinese point of view, when a venture is jointly managed, its ownership changes, and it can no longer 'eat out of the same big pot' or receive subsidies from the state should it incur losses, and greater efficiency is thereby promoted. In addition, the autonomy of joint ventures in the appointment and dismissal of employees as well as fixing wages breaks the old 'iron rice bowl' system of permanent tenure and generates greater enthusiasm among both management and workers.

With more efficient use of funds and a better educated workforce, foreign investors are in a good position to make the best use of imported technology and equipment. The foreign partner often has access to the kind of knowledge and hardware to update and improve products, and along with better management skills, this factor makes joint ventures more competitive in international markets. In addition, the business experience gained by Chinese personnel has a spin-off effect on other domestic enterprises because in time local factories will become involved in processing and acquiring local resources.

Although economic reforms have promoted the devolution of decision-making power to local bodies and individual enterprises, the state retains control over where joint ventures may be established. The key objective is to acquire knowledge and experience of the most advanced foreign industrial processes, even if current economic strategy demands that a balance be struck between upgrading existing plant and introducing new technologies. Target projects are as follows: advanced technologies and skills needed to develop new products; ventures which can help other enterprises in the same industry to carry out technical change; national resource development requiring large amounts of investment and imported technology, especially sectors like offshore oil and coal exploitation; and schemes to develop new varieties of export products for different foreign markets as well as to make possible more import substitution. Thus Chinese national interests come before sectional interests: foreign economic co-operation is encouraged in well-managed units but not in the best enterprises because, left alone, these will benefit from competing with joint ventures. This is one way of reducing the potential for foreign economic control. For national security reasons, too, foreign investments are forbidden in sectors like defence although, as in the COCOM debate concerning exports to China, it is often difficult in practice to distinguish between civilian and military technology.

The benefits of joint ventures for China are apparent but Western investors, mindful of past Chinese anti-colonialist rhetoric, are cautious. To reassure them, the Chinese government, early in 1986, updated the Law on Joint Ventures to the effect that foreign enterprises would not be nationalised or confiscated except in special circumstances relating to the Chinese national interest, and in such cases proper compensation would be made.

At the same time steps are being taken to improve the investment environment. In the early 1980s foreigners were complaining that the time-scale for joint ventures was too short to make their investments worthwhile, even though the Chinese had always accepted that such operations should be adjusted according to the equity stake, profit volume and capital recovery, on the principle that each party should expect to receive reasonable returns. Accordingly, in January 1986 The Regulations for the Implementation of the China-Foreign Joint Venture Law were amended in favour of greater foreign equity over a longer period. This includes a stipulation allowing enterprises with low returns, advanced technologies and international competitive power to operate for fifty years, with the possibility of further extension subject to the approval of the State Council.[12]

Although co-operation with EC countries is being undertaken across a broad sprectrum of China's economy, this study will focus upon the development priority sectors discussed above. China's modernisation programme is handicapped by poor transportation links, and these must be improved to meet the need for greater mobility of both freight and passengers. Agreements have paved the way for joint ventures in these sectors: witness the Sino-French agreement of May 1985, providing for co-operation in feasibility studies, and highway and expressway projects. Aspects covered include design, construction, work-site management and maintenance facilities. In addition, the Chinese are to receive the latest computer technology for road safety purposes.[13]

Expansion of the road network particularly into the countryside, offers further possibilities for joint-venture manufacturing. An agreement to establish a truck manufacturing business was signed in March 1985 by the Guangzhou Motor Vehicle Plant, the China International Trust and Investment Corporation, Peugeot of France and La Banque Nationale de Paris. Called the Guangzhou Peugeot Automobile Company, the venture is planned to last for twenty years, eventually building 50,000 mini-trucks a year. A proportion of the output will be exported to France but the remainder sold in China. With a cargo capacity of one ton, the truck is particularly suitable for rural transport, already increasing with the growth of industries in the Chinese countryside.[14]

To date the few cars in China have been officially owned rather than privately run but this pattern is slowly changing, with the growing wealth of entrepreneurs. To take advantage of this expanding market, in October 1984 Volkswagen signed a joint-venture agreement to produce a Santana model in Shanghai, the first of its kind between China and a foreign car maker.

China's waterways, a traditional means of transport but not utilised to the full, offer great potential and an area in which European expertise may be used to advantage. In May 1985 the Rhine-Meuse and Ocean Shipping Office, a German concern, together with Chinese partners, formed the Kiangsi Corporation: this was designed to share experience in the domain of inland and river-ocean shipping, hydraulic engineering and canal construction as well as port management, the main initial project being the construction of a ship fleet in the province of Kiangsi.

In the mid-1980s China's use of waterways was being constrained by inadequate shipping, and the German partners have had much experience in improving infrastructures in developing countries. The major feature of co-operation in this instance is the transfer of knowhow, which helps the Chinese build large carriers and barge container carriers, that is to say, transport ships capable of loading and delivery, these being best suited to China, a country with few harbour facilities. In addition, ship simulators, made in Germany, will assist in training Chinese personnel.[15]

Harbour construction is not being neglected, and under a Sino-French inland shipping agreement the two countries are co-operating in the building and management of river ports. The Chinese will also benefit from French expertise in navigation, telecommunications and safety control.

Energy is one of China's bottlenecks, and the Chinese are concentrating on exploiting their huge coal deposits through better machinery and technical imports from EC countries. Feasibility studies and the design of the Yuanbaoshan coalfield in the North-western province of Liaoning in co-operation with West Germany are recent examples. As of 1983, coal-fired plants accounted for 78 percent of thermal generating capacity, and although this pattern is unlikely to change substantially in the immediate future, oil and nuclear power have been gaining ground as alternative sources of energy. Many of the ambitious plans for economic development in the Southern coastal province of Guangdong and the subtropical island of Hainan are based on the expectation that oil and gas will be discovered. The French company, Total China, consented to trial production in a small oilfield in the South China Sea, although many experts doubt its commercial viability. As of 1985, other companies like British Petroleum had yet to find offshore resources of any magnitude. European co-operation in this sector, however, has been bedevilled by the harsh terms imposed by the Chinese partner, the China National Offshore Oil Corporation (CNOOC), whereby foreign companies pay for exploration and, after any discovery, at least 49 percent of the development costs. Moreover, oil and gas are priced at artificially low levels in China, and if co-operation is to continue the Chinese must raise the foreign share of revenues and offer rewards in line with effort and risk.

Nuclear power is increasingly being seen as a third energy option, and the Chinese have concluded nuclear power agreements with France in 1983 and Britain in 1985. In this context the Daya Bay nuclear power station is one of the largest joint investment projects undertaken since the beginning of China's economic 'open-door' policy. Initial investment, which was to account for 10 percent of overall construction projects, was funded from Guangdong provincial and Hong Kong sources; it is intended that the colony should have one-fifth of its electric power needs met by the plant on its completion in the early 1990s. The rest of the construction costs will be borne by the Guangdong Nuclear Power Joint Venture Company, (as the whole enterprise is called) in its capacity as a Chinese institution.[16]

By January 1986 agreement had been reached in principle on contracts for the operation of the nuclear power plant. Two French firms, together with one British company, agreed to supply the nuclear reactor generating equipment and project services, and General Electric of Britain signed a memorandum of understanding with China to provide two turbines.[17] All the signs are that the project, sited forty miles North-east of Hong Kong, will be completed even though, in Hong Kong, in 1986, a strong campaign against it was mounted on environmental grounds.

Quadrupling industrial output by the turn of the century will also depend on the exploitation of China's abundant mineral resources. In April 1983 the China Nonferrous Metals Industrial Corporation was set up, one of its main tasks being the promotion of technical exchanges with foreign firms. There have been several government-level accords on exploration and development projects, like that signed with France in July 1980 to prospect for tungsten and chromium in Xinjiang Province.

Joint ventures have not been confined to sectors like transportation, energy and mineral resources but have encompassed a wide range of other activities. These include two notable Sino-British joint ventures: the Shanghai Yaohua Pilkington Glass Company, projected to be one of the largest manufacturers of its kind in operation in China in 1986, and the Sino-British Printing Company in which Richard Clay, one of Britain's largest book printers, partners the China National Printing Corporation for both the Chinese and international markets. In 1985 a French brewing consortium signed an agreement with the Chinese (including the Chinese International Trust and Investment Corporation) establishing a joint venture to meet increasing Chinese domestic demand for beer and exports as well. In the context of China's economic reforms, foreign companies frequently cooperate with provincial departments, as has the Italian Factory Equipment Design Company which agreed in 1984 to set up joint investment tanneries and shoe factories in Sichuan, Anhui and Zhejiang.

While in the longer term the relatively underdeveloped inland provinces of China offer the greatest scope for investment—even if only Western multinationals or groups of companies would have the resources to cope with the daunting problems of accessibility—in the next four years the Chinese leaders envisage the Special Economic Zones as the main sites for foreign economic co-operation, on the principle that development on the coast will push progress in to the backward hinterland.

When designated in the early 1980s the Special Economic Zones were intended to promote the adoption of advanced manufacturing technology but this has proceeded rather slowly. The fastest to grow have been hotel construction, tourism and commerce although these are also seen as paving the way for other industries. Shenzhen, for example, was virtually a 'green-field' site when given zone status, and not surprisingly in 1984 almost 38 percent of the city's production was accounted for by construction work, manufacturing representing 34 percent and commerce and tourism a further 16 percent. Exports, at 34 percent of industrial output, still lag behind the target of 60 percent. These statistics are reflected in the nature of foreign investment in the zone.[18] As of the mid-1980s, much of China's joint ventures was located in the Special Economic Zones, even though EC participation was as yet not as great as that of Hong Kong and Japanese investors. One important European undertaking was an agreement, signed in 1985, to transfer Danish construction knowhow by Dangroup International which became the first consulting engineering firm to work with the Chinese Ministry of Housing and the Environment. In addition to Shenzhen, a major focus of the joint venture was to be in Dalian, an area being upgraded with housing, factories and roads with a view to turning the country's second most important port into a centre of foreign investment and technology. In time, following the example of the Special Zones, growing expectations of better housing for people living elsewhere in China could enable the European building industry to penetrate one of the world's largest markets.

Often in the past the Chinese leaders have undertaken pilot projects in limited areas before applying them to the country as a whole, and in many respects Special Economic Zones are intended as pace-setters. Their economic function has already been discussed but they also lead the way in providing amenities and welfare facilities. In adopting market policies for the Special Zones, the Chinese leaders have been able to experiment as with wage reforms, for instance, in collaboration with foreign partners. A case in point is the system by which foreign-affiliated enterprises in the Shekou industrial area of Shenzhen pay wages in foreign currencies to the labour corporation of the area's management commission. Of the total amount, 70 percent is paid to the workers directly by the corporation, and of the remaining 30 percent, 5 percent is allocated to welfare expenditure for the workers and 25 percent is deducted by the labour corporation for other purposes. Wages consist of a basic payment plus a performance-based increment, thereby offering a strong incentive to the work-force. There is also an additional 'floating' component of the wage which takes attitudes to work and labour quality into account. This ensures a good deal of flexibility, with the evaluation of a worker's performance linked to an enterprise's profits. This could prove useful since new employees in Shenzhen are often peasants who have no experience of industrial work discipline. These wage reforms may also go some way towards solving China's problem of low labour productivity in the rest of the country; this is essential if product quality and competitiveness are to be ensured on domestic and international markets.[19]

Through co-operation with foreign partners in joint ventures as well as with Western oil companies like British Petroleum in Shenzhen, the Chinese will acquire valuable experience in operating new personnel and wage systems as well as learning more about business management and professional training.

Although EC participation in the Chinese economy is still minor, as it grows it will bring not only material benefits to China but also cultural changes. China's leaders want to keep out those aspects of Western culture which they consider undesirable—constituting 'spiritual pollution'—but EC countries are already playing a key role in imparting the skills, attitudes and values of the modernisation process.

At present there are thousands of Chinese postgraduate students taking courses in Europe, and they are destined to become China's future Party and government leaders, entrepreneurs, captains of industry and research scientists. The largest group is studying in the Federal Republic of Germany, many of the students (expecially those in the natural sciences and technology) being on scholarships provided by the host government. In addition, in accordance with a Sino-German agreement of 1978, joint research projects in a number of technical areas like energy, metallurgy, electronics and machine tools have been initiated, to the benefit of enterprises in both countries. Thus Sino-European technological exchange is not a one-way process but the EC countries have nevertheless more to offer China in professional sectors like banking, law and management. These services will come into their own with the growing complexity of modern government and a more diversified economy.

Even more than manufacturing, the professions require changes in their philosophical content, attitudes and values, all of which are indispensable for a modern industrial economy. Prior to the reforms of the early 1980s, the command economy allocated resources and distributed products; the banks played a minor role and an independent legal profession was hardly necessary because state bodies adjudicated any disputes between or claims by enterprises, and factory directors and managers were effectively government employees. The devolution of decision-making powers together with the encouragement of entrepreneurs and market forces, not to mention provincial initiative in foreign trade, demand more sophisticated means of financial control, the codification of new laws and the training of lawyers.

As of the mid-1980s banks were yet to make any significant impact in China, even though many major European names had established their presence through representative offices, the main task of concerns like Lloyds being to help their own clients do business with China. The days when it would be possible to open retail banking branches throughout China seemed a long way off. There were, however, some significant developments, one of which was an agreement between the Bank of China and ten foreign banks from seven countries to issue bonds in West Germany. The management of the bond issue—designed to enable the Bank of China to draw on foreign capital for China's modernisation programme—was led by the Deutsche Bank in collaboration with Kleinwort Benson of Britain and Banque Nationale de Paris of France.[20]

Similarly, also in 1985, West Germany's second biggest commercial bank, Dresdner, entered into partnership with the Bank of China which agreed to set up a joint venture with foreign banks within China itself. The enterprise, called the China Universal Leasing Company, was also to engage in the importation of advanced knowhow in fields like computers and telecommunications for Chinese enterprises. Dresdner was to have a 23 percent stake in the venture, the rest of the capital being held by the Sanwa Bank of Japan and the Bank of China along with three Chinese foreign trade organisations. Dresdner Bank officials envisaged that the venture would further their business in China, involving as it did trade finance and the raising of loans for Chinese organisations.[21]

Inseparable from the financial component of these agreements is the potential for assisting Chinese personnel to familiarise themselves with international banking practice. In 1985 the Dutch Rotterdam-Amsterdam Farmers' Bank contracted to train Chinese staff in the Netherlands, and similar arrangements were already in force between Chinese and West German banks.[22]

Like Western-style banking, insurance in China is in its infancy, although Chinese authorities took steps in the mid-1980s to launch the profession by allowing Chinese organisations with a given amount of assets to set up an insurance business. Because of their location and economic strength, cities like Shanghai were obvious centres for insurance operations. These developments hold out lucrative reinsurance business for firms like Lloyds which can also impart their expertise to Chinese personnel.

The moves towards creating a legal system in the 1980s have not meant the birth of an independent judiciary but nevertheless they do start to provide framework within which domestic and foreign economic relations can work; furthermore, Western investors must be assured that their stake in joint ventures is safe from expropriation by future Chinese governments. Since 1980 a number of Chinese industrial and mining enterprises have been employing lawyers—though they are still in short supply, full-time members of the profession numbering less than 9,000 in 1984. The Chinese have also given guarantees on foreign patents by acceding to the Paris Treaty on Intellectual Property in March 1985. Taking a broader perspective, China still does not have case law like that found in Britain or America, and negotiators regard the relationship between Notes of Agreement and Contracts, for example, in a different light from their Western counterparts: thus Notes of Agreement are seen as virtually binding by the Chinese rather than just a prelude to more discussions. Perhaps the Chinese, through sending personnel for legal training in Europe and through more experience in negotiation, will in time move closer to Western legal practice.

The command economy has also left its mark on the Chinese industrial management system, and foreign partners in joint ventures have often complained of low labour productivity which has often reduced profit margins in spite of low wage levels. As the system of life-tenured employment is discarded, the motivation of the work-force must be promoted by better trained managers. This, however, is not simply a matter of implanting Western attitudes in China as effective management is often the result of interaction between businesses and cultural factors. Other Asian countries like Japan and Singapore have used the Confucian group ethos to facilitate collective decision-making, thereby ensuring harmonious management-worker relations. In similar vein recent Chinese sources have asserted that the ancient philosophers of China's classical period understood the principles of what is now regarded as modern Western management; Japanese techniques, especially, are said to share the Confucian tradition. As in the case of European technology, the Chinese will adopt Western management techniques selectively, blending them with China's native experience and conditions.[23]

Nevertheless the Chinese admit that they have much to learn from their EC counterparts. As of 1984, for instance, there were only two institutions—the Dalian Management Institute and the Overseas Chinese University in Canton—with business and economics courses internationally acknowledged to be up to Western standards. Accordingly, to satisfy the increasing demand for skilled managers, it was announced in 1985 that a new business school would be built in Beijing, a project sponsored jointly by the Chinese government and the EC Commission, (through its overseas aid programme). Designed to train a business élite through a Master's degree programme under the auspices of the China Enterprise Management Association—itself part of the State Economic Commission—the school's courses follow the 'Manchester model' in combining academic and practical approaches. In the immediate term, however, China's shortage of well-trained management personnel can be made good only by the use of high technology in industry. Meanwhile graduates of the Beijing School will develop teaching materials for distance-learning programmes which will draw upon the experience of Britain's Open University Business School.[24]

These developments have brought in their train new methods of staff recruitment, particularly in the Special Economic Zones, where the majority of Chinese managers are now employed only after responding to advertisements and passing written and oral examinations—and not through the old system of state assignment. While much of China's industrial establishment is yet to feel the full impact of recent economic reforms, the encouragement of private enterprise and individual entrepreneurship, as well as the gradual introduction of Western legal norms, professional ethics and business management practice, are already creating a new social climate which is favourable to the attainment of the Four Modernisations.

4
Japan-EC Trade: Current Trends and Future Prospects

Few would have predicted after her defeat and devastation in 1945 that by the 1970's Japan would have become the second greatest economic power in the free world, enjoying massive trade surpluses with both Western Europe and the USA. Even though Japan played a role in international trade before World War II, her exports, especially her textile goods, were not highly regarded, whereas since the end of the war her products have gained a reputation for high quality and their prices have been so competitive that it has been possible to transport them to Europe at a profit. A number of reasons have been offered for this performance but it is claimed here that it has been due to a combination of factors, namely, Japan's traditional social values and cohesion, industrial power inherited from the pre-war period, American assistance and fortuitous international economic circumstances. As the Japanese economy 'took off' during the 1960's, benefiting from plentiful raw materials and oil supplies from the Third World, Japan's exports grew—and trading was more and more with the developed countries of the EC and the USA which could afford to import sophisticated consumer goods. The 1973 oil crisis was but a temporary setback, with Japan stressing energy conservation and increasing her competitive edge *vis-à-vis* other advanced industrial countries. By the mid 1970's Japan's trade surpluses with the EC showed a general upward trend; after a rough balance in 1970, the figures were in Japan's favour by US\$2 billion in 1974, just over US\$2 billion in 1975, US\$3.6 billion in 1976, US\$5 billion in 1977, US\$6 billion in 1978 and US\$7 billion in 1979. This trend has been maintained in the 1980s, witness Japanese surpluses with the EC of US\$10 billion in 1980, US\$14 billion in 1981, US\$12 billion in 1984, US\$11.5 billion in 1985, and US\$18 billion in 1986.[1] Thus, in 1986, in spite of the previous year's revaluation of the yen, there was still little, if any, sign of a reduction in the EC's adverse trade balance with Japan. Although a Japanese ambassador was not appointed to the EC until the late 1970s—thereby underlining the economic and political importance of the Community—Japan continued to capitalise on the differing approaches of European countries towards what were considered unfair Japanese trading practices. That the EC countries failed to take concerted action sprang from their varied cultural traditions and economic conditions.

In recent years Japanese trade names like Honda, Nissan, Hitachi and Sony have become household words in Europe and bear witness to Japanese supremacy in sectors such as cars, colour televisions sets and video recorders—of which an estimated nine out of ten sold in Western Europe in 1985 were made in Japan—as well as 35mm cameras, electronic calculators and motorcycles. While not exhaustive, this list indicates the range of Japanese penetration of EC markets. During the late 1970's and early 1980's individual EC countries varied in their responses to trade deficits with Japan; despite an adverse balance, though not as large as that of other EC countries, West Germany remained more committed than others to free trade but the British, French and Italians put pressure on the Japanese to restrict their exports (for instance, of cars) on a voluntary basis. In France's case the issue was particularly stark, as electronic products accounted for more than one-third of the French trade deficit with Japan in 1981 and yet France's exports of similar goods to Japan at that time represented only 6 percent of Japan's exports to France. At one stage French feeling ran so high that it was decided to channel all Japanese video tape recorders through one small customs post (Poitiers) so as to slow down the numbers imported. It is Japanese targeting of certain types of consumer goods that has drawn most criticism from EC governments, a case in point being the penetration of the popular end of the car market which led the British government to insist on quota ceilings limiting Japanese sales to 11 percent of total sales in the early 1980's.[2] During these years individual EC countries ran up considerable deficits with Japan, though Britain's US$2 to 3 billion was more than offset by invisible exports such as tourism, insurance, and shipping.

While differing approaches among individual EC countries allowed the Japanese to play one off against the other, by the mid-1980's the governments were more united in the face of Japan's trade onslaught. The Japanese have always been more responsive to the demands of US trade lobbies, especially in view of Nixon's moves against Japanese textiles in the early 1970's—and also because Japan relies on American imports of certain foodstuffs as well as raw materials. While this appears a classic developed-developing country relationship, other factors—like Japan's defence relationship with the USA—make the Japanese wary of antagonising powerful American pressure groups. In fact, Japanese concessions to the USA have often been at the expense of the EC countries. While it is only in recent years that exports have come to play an important role in Japan's economy, they are now crucial to help pay for imports of raw materials. In spite of Japan's major role in world trade, manufactured goods were only 22 percent of her total imports in the early 1980's, a figure substantially less than other modern industrial countries; the percentages for the EC and the USA were 44 and 54 respectively.[3] Moreover, by that time, while Japan's imports from the USA were increasing, those from the EC were declining.

Early on in 1983 Japanese diplomatic negotiators acceded to export restraints at Community level—whereas previously they had only acted to meet the complaints of individual member countries—and EC ministers welcomed the resulting agreement limiting some Japanese exports of video equipment, television sets and other high-tech products.

Nevertheless two examples indicate the EC's continuing concern at what was regarded as the unfair advantages enjoyed by Japanese goods. In December 1984 a duty of 43 percent was imposed on Japanese electronic typewriters after an anti-dumping investigation concluded that all manufacturers in Japan had been selling at less than economic cost to the EC, thereby undermining the profitability of Community industries and in turn reducing the funds for further research and development. In late 1985, a report published by the University of East Anglia Motor Industry Research Unit pointed to stagnating European production during the previous decade at a time when Japanese car imports trebled. Incentives like tax cuts to make local cars cheaper to run as well as more rigorous testing of used cars were suggested as possible measures to stem the tide of factory closures and reduced employment. Further retrenchment in the industry would, it was explained, reduce profits, making it more difficult for manufacturers to invest in automation and advanced technology which would enable them to react rapidly to future demand.[4]

By the mid-1980's, aware of the economic as well as social costs of high unemployment, EC governments concluded that concerted action was called for against Japan—if necessary through international bodies—in a world of increasing economic interdependence. Rectifying the EC-Japan trade imbalance, however, was not only a matter of curbing excessive Japanese imports but of penetrating the Japanese market. In December 1986, for example, EC negotiators rejected as inadequate Japanese offers to reduce taxes on imported wines and spirits and threatened to take the dispute to GATT; concessions on this symbolic issue would, it was believed, improve European chances of prising open the Japanese market to other products. To the EC leaders a clear instance of Japanese discrimination against the Community was the system of excise duty, twice as high on imported whisky as on the local variety; this meant at the time that Scotch whisky cost the equivalent of £60 a bottle in Japan.

Thus, whereas in the past the EC response to Japanese import penetration of the Community was to rely mainly on voluntary export constraints and anti-dumping petitions, by the mid-1980's a new approach emphasised multilateral negotiations and attempts at better co-ordination of national policies through bodies like GATT. Moves in this direction also stemmed from fears that agreements reached between the Japanese and the USA on market sharing—like that relating to semi-conductors in 1986—could be at the expense of EC manufacturers. The stress was also on opening up the Japanese market sector by sector and more horizontal trade whereby advanced industrial countries sell to each other similar kinds of manufactured goods, though differing in design or style; but this system can only work if there is equal access to markets. With some justice, EC countries have long complained of high Japanese tariff barriers, even though by the early 1980's a number of these had already been removed. In January 1983, to stave off the threat of protectionism abroad, the Japanese Cabinet reduced some tariffs and abolished others on 47 agricultural and 28 industrial goods, many of which had been originally imposed to protect Japanese manufacturers from foreign competition when the economy was being rehabilitated in the early post-war years. After further market-opening measures in 1985 tariffs on most manufactured imports had been removed, even though the ruling Liberal Democratic Party (LDP) continued to give greater protection to the agricultural sector. But EC countries have not been averse to restrictions on trade from outside the EC. In the early 1980's, even though

Japan's Ministry of International trade and Industry (MITI) welcomed the EC's decision to abolish certain discriminatory import restrictions aimed at Japan, Japanese diplomats claimed that other quotas against Japanese products had not been lifted.

The ability to penetrate foreign markets may be impeded by factors other than tariffs and EC negotiators have often accused the Japanese of using non-tariff barriers to protect their producers—witness, for instance, the anti-pollution legislation, more rigorous than in the EC and the USA and applied to imported cars. While by the mid-1980's the Japanese had gone some way towards reducing obstacles to the penetration of their markets—as shown by measures to simplify lengthy and complicated customs inspection procedures for imported goods as well as the addition of an advisory committee to Japan's trade ombudsman system—European suspicion lingers that Japanese governments collude with powerful manufacturers' lobbies to keep down foreign competition.

But while being willing to accommodate EC views, the Japanese have criticised Europeans for their poor marketing efforts. By early 1984, for example, Japanese companies had about five times as many offices in Britain as their counterparts in Japan, and there were about 4,000 Japanese commercial personnel working in Britain compared with fewer than 200 Britons in Japan. The Japanese were also linguistically better than the British, although this is slowly changing as evidenced by the growth of Japanese studies in British and other European universities.

In summary, since the early 1980's EC national leaders have increasingly seen the need to act in concert at both Community and international levels to protect themselves against what they regard as a Japanese threat to their prosperity. The Japanese themselves have become aware that in economic terms the concept of the nation-state is outmoded, and that their country's prosperity and enhanced position in international affairs bring with them a responsibility towards the well-being of both developed and developing countries. It is in any case not in the interests of traders to bankrupt their customers, and the Japanese know that for one country to build up large trade surpluses could open the flood gates of protectionism. In mid-1985 Prime Minister Nakasone, under the gaze of television cameras, made a public gesture of goodwill by buying foreign goods in a Tokyo department store to encourage others to follow his example and pave the way for more imports from the EC and the USA. Ever since their first close contacts with Europe in the mid-nineteenth century the Japanese have sought to acquire Western tastes and there is no reason why imports of Western consumer goods should not increase, what with the recent revaluation of the yen and as tariff and non-tariff barriers are lifted. Prospects for the sale of other EC products are also promising. Thus, richer Japanese can now afford expensive European cars; in 1984, although building on a small base—as the market for imported vehicles in Japan was still very small compared to the demand for Japanese models—Austin Rover of Britain increased its exports by 25 percent over the previous year. Other sectors also offer opportunities. Thus, while Japan's aircraft industry has considerable potential for development, there is a growing market for European planes; witness a contract won by British Aerospace for the sale of ten A340 Airbuses to All-Nippon Airways of Japan in late 1986.[5]

Having discussed the EC-Japan connection from the 1970's to the mid-1980's, the future of that relationship must now be assessed within the perspective of Japan's so-called post-war economic miracle. While Japan has risen in the world economic league, other Western countries have fallen back—though the EC, as one of the world's strongest regional blocs, could become a much greater force to be reckoned with and more powerful than the sum of its individual member states. Perhaps predictably, as a former enemy of the West, Japan has been criticised for enjoying unfair advantages, notably the 'free ride' on defence. Ironically, it was the Americans—through the Supreme Commander of the Allied Powers—who insisted on Article IX in the 1946 Japanese Constitution which forbade Japan maintaining a war potential (though this did not preclude the right of Self-Defence). In the wake of the Cold War, however, it was again the USA which put pressure on the Japanese to turn the Police Reserve (which had been designed to deal with internal insurrection) into an instrument for defence against external attack, and then to transform it into a proper army, navy and air force. As leaders of a trading nation, Japanese governments were reluctant to offend potential customers, and wished to develop as many markets and sources of supply as possible world-wide. They were especially anxious to remove any suspicion of Japan's motives in South-east Asia, which provided raw materials for Japan's growing economy, particularly in view of Japan's war record. These factors put a brake on rearmament and the pace was never fast enough for American policymakers.

In 1976, under the Miki administration, it was decided to limit

defence spending to one per cent of the national income and
although this was a considerable amount in total, there was growing resentment in the Western alliance that the Japanese were
having a 'free ride' as far as defence was concerned, and consequently could devote more attention to competitive economic
and trade policies.

By 1986, however, the increased Soviet threat in the Pacific,
combined with American pressure concerning Japan's trade surpluses, led the Nakasone Cabinet to breach the one per cent
limit on defence. Since the early 1980's the Japanese had also
begun to take greater responsibility for the defence of the Japanese islands and sealanes, and Western complaints about Japanese
unwillingness to carry their share of the allied defence burden
were growing less valid.

We must therefore look elsewhere to explain Japan's post-war
trading success, and in particular to Japan's cultural traditions,
social values and economic structure. Social and economic trends
need to be identified along with their implications for Japan-EC
trade and economic co-operation in the future.

Japan has become known as one of the few successful modernisers and examples of democratic governments in the non-
Western world. No single reason, but a complex of factors,
can be proposed to explain Japan's rise to one of the foremost
world powers during a little more than a hundred years. In
the wake of the Western colonial onslaught of the mid-nineteenth
century, the Japanese, unlike the Chinese, maintained their
country's independence. The early introduction of conscription
and reform of the education system helped to promote patriotism
and thus achieve national unity; the creation of a legal system
as a framework for economic growth and social stability made
possible the rapid recovery of tariff autonomy. But although
Japan had many features in common with other countries in
Asia and Africa, she was in some respects the exception that
proved the rule. Her population was homogeneous with few
ethnic minorities—in contrast with, say, the tribalism of African
countries—and in spite of an inadequate modern transport and
communications system, a long period of internal peace and
political unity had brought socio-economic changes, similar to
those that had taken place during the breakdown of feudalism
in Europe just before the industrial revolution. Gradually, over
the previous two centuries, the Samurai, the old warrior class,
had become administrators serving their lords in the castle towns,
and new specialist skills and professional values had developed,

providing an appropriate philosophical infrastructure—that is to say, the values and attitudes conducive to the modernisation process which began in earnest after 1868. With the Meiji Restoration the Emperor was restored to power as the symbol of the nation, although his position later became more akin to that of a constitutional monarch. He thus represented a powerful focus of loyalty and one in whose name policies to strengthen Japan could be initiated. From the outset the Meiji oligarchs (as the new government leaders came to be known) sought to adopt Western industrial and technical skills to enable Japan to be able to compete with the colonial powers on their own terms, as only in this way could Japan's independence be preserved. Prior to the Meiji Restoration Japan had been divided into a number of fiefdoms, and the familial-group type loyalties to feudal lords introduced the Japanese to the idea of international relations and of competing nation-states. Thus while foreign experts were welcomed to Japan to impart their expertise in various fields, Western economic influence was strictly supervised by government against the danger of foreign domination. Moreover, the Japanese, relative latecomers to the industrial revolution, were in a position to obtain the latest technology.

Big merchant houses were inherited from the pre-Meiji period but the initiative of government played a key role in blazing the trail to industrial modernity. In the early Meiji years the government helped to lay a physical infrastructure for the economy but even more importantly it was the prime mover in developing certain industries which were then sold on easy terms to business interests. In addition, the commuted stipends of the Samurai, a group deprived of its previous function by law after 1868, helped to provide investment funds. A connection with the old ruling classes was thus retained but also created was a link between Japanese government and business which persists today to an extent unknown in other free enterprise economies. This must be seen as a major factor in the emergence of Japan as an industrial power before World War II.

Prior to 1945 Japan could not have been considered a democracy as we understand the term in the West but there was a public consensus on the methods necessary to create a strong Japan. Political parties did exist—based on groups from former Samurai left out of the ruling oligarchy during the early Meiji period—but their interests were poorly articulated and their popular bases narrow. In any case they could only form cabinets in co-operation with powerful bureaucratic lobbies, the armed forces and others who competed in their loyalty to the Emperor. Thus the influence of political parties over national policy was rather circumscribed, and as defence ministers had to be serving officers, the military could bring down cabinets at will by refusing to put forward names for appointment. However, militarism did not destroy the powerful link between government and business even when business people were not always united behind the war effort.

There are, of course, various ways of reaching a general national consensus. The 1946 Japanese Constitution—imposed by the USA and an amalgam of Anglo-American principles—created a political system and electoral laws which envisaged the alternation of political parties in government and opposition. In practice, however, Japan has had not a two-party but a one-and-a-half-party system, and apart from a brief socialist-led coalition administration in 1947 and 1948, the conservative LDP in its various forms has been re-elected again and again to government. The survival of traditional Japanese values of hierarchy and social cohesion have contributed most to Japan's economic development goals since 1945; the LDP, being a collection of personal factions and pressure groups, has represented a wide range of interests across the social and economic spectrum. In addition, well coordinated national planning is facilitated by the close personal links between politicians, bureaucrats and businessmen.

Reference has already been made to the Meiji oligarchy's measures to preserve Japan's independence, both politically and economically, and this attitude also informed the creation of the country's financial system. This was not much linked to foreign financial markets but was used to direct the country's resources into priority sectors. Interest rates were fixed by the Ministry of Finance for the banks and by the Ministry of Posts and Telecommunications for Post Office savings. These funds were then channelled into the development of strategic industries. The financial system was thus a closed one; savers had the disadvantage of controlled interest rates but the benefit of government patronage, as the banks could not fail. Consequently, no real securities market developed on Western lines.

The close relationship between Japanese government and business together with a financial system that was closed to foreign participation continued in the post-1945 period. (Recent moves towards financial deregulation and internationalisation are discussed later on). Undoubtedly, these features have contributed to Japan's economic success. Just as Western-type political institutions, as outlined in the 1946 Constitution, have been informed by traditional Japanese social values, so also have economic institutions been given Japanese content. Because of their ambivalent attitude to previous Japanese international expansion, the zaibatsu or financial cliques—dominated at their highest levels by certain families—were seen by the American Occupation authorities as undesirable concentrations of economic power which had reflected and fuelled the authoritarianism of the 1930s. Accordingly, the zaibatsu were broken up, the old families and their holding companies removed from control and anti-monopoly laws passed. As a result, progressive middle-ranking salaried employees, orientated towards growth of market share, rose to prominence. In time, however, reconcentration took place, encouraged in part by changes in Occupation policy in the wake of the Cold War, as Japan was increasingly seen as a bastion against Communism in Asia and economic strength as an aid to political stability and national security. These groupings have since come to be known as keiretsu or linkages—though now primarily directed by banks and trading companies rather than the old families, the most famous being the familiar pre-war names of Mitsubishi, Mitsui and Sumitomo. Superficially, these would appear to be Western-type monopolies but the fact that they are active in virtually all major industries creates fierce competition, especially on the Japanese market, and this has placed them in a good position to win export battles in other countries.

The Japanese have become known for their ability to adapt to the vagaries of economic events at home and abroad, and this is in no small part due to the keiretsu which, by their size and wealth, can invest considerable capital in new ventures; even during downturns in international trade they are able to continue research and development as well as create new productive capacity, thus giving them the edge against foreign competitors. In fact, Japanese economic decision-making has been willing to take a long-term view and this is reflected in how industry is financed. Although the Japanese have one of the busiest Stock Exchanges in the world, it is not so much through the capital market as the banking system that funds are channelled to industry. Management priority is to increase market share by developing new products, ensuring high quality and cutting costs; in other words, a long view is taken as opposed to the short-term in other economic systems where stock markets are more dominant. Moreover, because until 1986 the Japanese government controlled interest rates, Japan's industries enjoyed cheaper capital funds

than their competitors abroad. Partly due to the slow growth
of state-run welfare services and pension schemes, ordinary Japanese had a high propensity to save and most of their savings
were placed in Japan's Post Office which could offer savers a
better yield than the banks were allowed to offer. Those funds
were invested in projects governments deemed to be strategic
to Japan's future economic development, and this helped industry to progress.

There were other ways, too, in which the state helped to create
a favourable environment for business. Ever since the Meiji Restoration the bureaucracy has enjoyed great prestige in the eyes
of the Japanese public who trust it to determine policy in the
national interest. This, together with the long electoral domi-
nance of one political party, the LDP, has often permitted
decision-making in areas of public policy without much political
controversy. Important as institutional mechanisms through
which bureaucrats, businessmen, experts and other public figures
consult over public policy are the deliberative councils, a number
of which are organized by Ministries like Finance and International Trade and Industry; these create a sense of economic direction, often lacking in Western countries. A similar body, the
Tax System Investigation Council, has been notable for recom-
mending 'tax breaks' for infant industries.

The Japanese are known for improving upon technology purchased from abroad, and in the early years of post-war recovery,
patents and licences were obtained from US companies. But by
the 1970's Japanese governments were promoting research and
development in Japan through funding and collaboration with
Japanese industry. To ensure co-ordination and prevent any duplication of effort, the Ministry of International Trade and Industry (MITI) set up research cartels to help competing firms
collaborate on specific projects which also advance Japan's technology as a whole. So often in the last decade the Japanese
have been adept at selecting winners, with attention focused on
areas such as microelectronics, biotechnology and telecommunications. The new 'technopolises' or science cities, like Tsukuba,
where many research laboratories established under the auspices
of MITI have been located, both reflect and are intended to
promote the new social and economic structures demanded by
the new technologies.[6]

This national industrial strategy has enabled the Japanese to
remain competitive internationally. In the early post-war years
the Japanese placed stress on traditional products like textiles

and then moved on to heavy and chemical industries as well as shipbuilding. As world trade patterns changed and newly industrialising countries enjoyed the advantage of cheap labour, Japan's industrialists moved some of their production to countries like Taiwan and South Korea. In time, the country began to appear more suited to the electronics industries and by the 1980's Japan had become the world's leader in certain areas of computers and robotics. It is this ability to think ahead that has fuelled Japan's successful export drive, though the part played by human relations in the smooth running of industry is not to be undervalued. The premium placed upon consensus, hierarchy and group loyalty in Japan must to some degree explain the country's good labour relations. A great deal has been made by Western observers of the lifetime employment system in Japan and remuneration and promotion on the basis of seniority, as well as co-operative trade unions as crucial factors in Japan's economic success. These can be discussed in the general context of management-labour relations.

The term 'trade union' is a misnomer when applied to Japan because in the post-war period these have been organised within individual enterprises—they are not based on craft, trade or industry—and they cover both blue and white-collar workers. Moreover, as the union structure frequently parallels the company's executive hierarchy and there is regular consultation between the two sides, a community of interest develops. Workers gain a strong sense of identity with a company; their union representatives are informed of the firm's financial standing and do not normally make wage claims which they know the company cannot afford to meet. Although wages have been kept within bounds; however, they have been high enough to permit increased personal consumption, and a strong domestic market has helped to make Japanese exports competitive. The national union federations, to which many unions are affiliated, have been concerned with political rather than purely economic matters, although their weight has been used to achieve wage parity across industries.

This picture is rather an idealised one, and certainly the decentralised nature of unions makes the survival of paternalism more likely. Yet the system has benefited the work-force in guaranteeing not only wage increases but a lifetime tenure of employment, although by the mid-1980's there were signs of greater labour mobility. Japanese firms tend not to dismiss staff in times of economic downturn but to redeploy staff to other parts of the organisation. On their part, the trade unions have served to defuse labour unrest and thus foster economic stability.

Lifetime tenure of employment along with welfare benefits like medical care and facilities for sport and social functions give a sense of security and commitment to the work-force. It should be noted, however, that only a small proportion of the country's labour belongs to trade unions covering full-time workers in the larger industrial concerns. Temporary workers in major industries as well as many employees in small companies are not unionised, and these can be more easily dismissed and do not enjoy as many welfare benefits and privileges. During times of recession the ability of the major companies to dismiss temporary workers provides management with the necessary flexibility to adjust to fluctuating markets.

The Japanese have always had great respect for age and group concensus and this would seem at first sight to militate against rewarding individuals on merit. As it has been unusual for individuals to move to other companies, age and seniority in a firm have been closely correlated. Salaries rise sharply according to years of service but, of course, only a minority of individuals can rise to top positions. Moreover although the pattern is changing, manages and workers have normally been recruited separately and it is then difficult to cross the white-collar/blue-collar boundary. Generally speaking, however, salary increases only become important after seven year's employment with the firm, though they grow rapidly after that. The restructuring of industry during rapid technological change may well accelerate the trend towards greater stress on merit than seniority in determining wages. But even now the two most important factors in salary rises are effectiveness as a manager and the prosperity of the company. Over and above their basic pay, Japanese employees receive bonus payments twice a year equal to between two and six months salary, and individuals may therefore be rewarded for their performance without compromising the seniority-based salary system. (In many firms young employees of two or three years standing are secretly selected, placed on the elite track and later given difficult assignments). While bonuses are not publicly vaunted—so as to save face for others not so privileged—they are (in addition to faster promotion) a means of rewarding exceptional merit. Moreover, as the number of new entrants to enterprises declines, so the trend towards stress on individual capability as opposed to age in determining wages will be accentuated.

Individual merit is also a key factor in promotion within Japanese industrial and business enterprises, even though it must also be seen in the context of group consensus, an important feature of corporate decision-making in Japan. Many observers have pointed to the elitist and hierarchical nature of Japanese society, especially as reflected in the education system and the universities. It is from these that large corporations recruit their executives and the prestige of a newcomer's university is itself an indicator of future progress. Recent studies, however, have indicated that no entrants may rest on their academic 'laurels', and their performance in the early years of employment is closely monitored for promotion purposes, a crucial determinant being relationships with superiors.[7] Decision-making in Japan is carried out within groups of executives to a much greater extent than in Western countries, and so a manager must be a good team person as well as an individual high flier. Companies also implement a job rotation system whereby managers are seconded to various departments of a firm for substantial periods, the purpose being to develop well-rounded generalists better equipped to make decisions in the interests of the company as a whole rather than just those of particular parts of the business. Job rotation is also intended to promote corporate unity of purpose as managers develop close personal ties throughout the company. Thus in the award of promotion a broad view of the company's affairs is more important than achievement *per se*. In-house educational programmes serve a similar function.[8]

The essence of effective leadership is to get employees to accept a command or course of action without incurring their resentment. The development of a community of interest and *esprit de corps* between executives and the work-force has long been cited as one reason for the success of Japanese management. Along with government leadership and business strategy, cultural inputs have been crucial, and it remains to be seen whether these can be successfully transferred to EC countries and emulated by those in charge of ailing industries. The adoption of certain features of Japanese management practice outside Japan will be examined later on in the context of economic co-operation with the EC.

By the mid-1980s Japanese leaders were becoming more aware that their country's prosperity would only be maintained by acknowledging the 'interdependence' of the world's major economies and the need to restructure Japan's economy in view of its trade surpluses. During the 1970s and mid-1980s growth in Japan's national income had come more from foreign trade than from domestic demand such as government spending or private consumption. In 1985 and 1986 financial and economic measures were already being taken by the Japanese, though admittedly under Western pressure, to boost domestic sales of consumer goods and, through yen revaluation, raise the prices of Japanese exports. In 1985 the yen was allowed to float to levels appropriate to Japan's economic strength, and by early 1987 the exchange rate was at an all-time high. While there were as yet only tentative signs of reduced export surpluses, Japanese competitiveness was already declining because of higher prices following the revaluation of the yen. There were other trends moving in the same direction; because of higher labour costs the Japanese were less able to compete with some of the newly industrialising countries in some sectors, and with a better educated population Japan was now more suited to high-tech activities. Domestic demand was also being fuelled by cheaper commodity imports, and local industries also benefited from less expensive raw materials and energy.

Earlier in 1986 the Maekawa Report, prepared by an officially-established committee of leading financiers and industrialists under the leadership of a former Governor of the Bank of Japan, called for a shift from export-led to domestic-led growth, and Mr Nakasone later assured EC politicians that its recommendations would be implemented. But even though these measures were the most thoroughgoing to date and went some way towards assuaging the doubts of EC leaders, it was clear that they could only be sustained in the long term by far-reaching fiscal and economic changes.

The reform of Japan's taxation system, for instance, is long overdue. As observers have so often pointed out, although Japan has the world's second highest national income, public amenities like housing and sanitation fall far below Western standards. One reason for this has been Japan's budgetary deficit—running in 1985 at about four per cent of national income—which inhibits government spending on public works as a means of stimulating the economy, a measure which would not only improve living conditions but provide employment for those made redundant in the heavy industrial sectors. A root cause of deficits in the past had been a tax system which fell heavily on large corporations and their salaried employees but favoured the self-employed and farmers who came to enjoy higher average salaries as a result. Furthermore, Japanese land scheduled for farming had been taxed more lightly than housing, and so owners were reluctant to sell land for development.[9] Acknowledging these anomalies, in 1985 the government announced an increase in expenditure on public works, and the tax on housing was reduced. In December 1986 the Nakasone government outlined its tax reform programme, which included cuts in both individual and corporate tax rates. To recoup and increase revenue a value-added tax of about five per cent on most goods and services was proposed, together with higher levies on interest earned on savings, previously exempt from tax. There is always the danger, of course, that indirect taxes, while creating a more equitable tax system, could dampen domestic demand for Japanese products and imports.

These adjustments must be seen in conjunction with other provisions of the 1987 budget. Only expenditure on defence and overseas aid—both up by a little over 5 per cent—increased significantly, and little stimulus was provided for domestic demand, dashing hopes at the time that the Japanese would lead the Western world out of recession. The shift from exports to imports was nevertheless given some impetus; loans for imports and investment finance were planned to rise but those for exports reduced.[10] This was but the latest in a series of measures to boost purchases from abroad; earlier, in 1983, the government's Export-Import Bank had reduced the interest rate range for import credits in relation to manufactured goods.

In the years to come, measures like the above—as well as the practice of retraining and redeploying workers with redundant skills within their own company—are likely to give way to the more fundamental shifts in employment required by the new high-technology industries. In the early 1970s and early 1980s Japanese export surpluses stemmed from the penetration of EC mass markets for consumer goods; current trends suggest the Japanese will move away from these and concentrate on more specialist products. It was suggested earlier that one of the keys to Japan's economic success has been adaptability to changing trends. Again Japanese business is taking a long-term view and investing in plant and equipment independent of the business cycle, the major stress this time being on technological innovation. Thus Japanese management, motivated towards economic growth, is expanding human as well as physical capacity ahead of demand, with emphasis on the development of personal creativity. Increasingly, the Japanese economy will have a software orientation, the service industries as well as banking and insurance playing a growing role. These trends will be reflected in Japan's foreign trade pattern: raw material imports will be replaced by medium-technology commodities, and manufacturing exports by high value-added products.

In the wake of this reorientation will come social changes to disprove the old catch phrase that the Japanese are merely 'economic animals', sacrificing personal comfort and leisure for a high national income. Nevertheless, if the Japanese are to retain their prosperity, help rectify trade imbalances and promote aid programmes for developing countries, then they must sustain a high growth rate, led basically by expanding domestic demand. Moreover, though the rest of this century will see more elderly people in Japan, the country's age structure is still relatively young and can thus maintain a high savings rate. In post-war Japan there has been a strong tradition of saving among both young and old. This could well continue and facilitate the setting of government priorities which will therefore not only include boosting domestic demand but the creation of more social capital—major emphasis being on housing, urban renewal and public works.

In concentrating on high-technology sectors, the Japanese are closing down 'smokestack' industries or moving them overseas. This shift could mean lower industrial demand for energy, and thus for domestically-produced coal. Mining in Japan is inefficient and heavily subsidised by the government, and as the price of local coal is twice that of foreign coal, imports are a better long-term proposition.

In the past agriculture too has enjoyed heavy subsidies from the taxpayer largely because LDP governments have had to attend to a powerful farming lobby, much to the chagrin of foreign producers who accuse the Japanese of being even more protectionist in this than in the industrial sector. Post-war dietary changes and consumer preference point towards greater consumption of foreign foods which are often cheaper than local ones. Reduced agricultural acreage also makes sense in a country short of land for housing and new industries.

These economic changes place a premium on entrepreneurial and innovative skills, and as some manufacturing sectors decline, employment will increase in knowledge-intensive fields like research and development. The trend towards shorter working hours—encouraged by the government to reduce exports and create a market for imports—is likely to accelerate, especially in high-technology sectors which by their nature demand greater flexibility of work practices. Any resultant rise in costs will be met by more investment in automation. The Japanese have often stressed the virtues of conformity, particularly through their education system, but creative ability in science and technology calls for a more Western-style individualist attitude, with career paths tailored more to particular needs and abilities.

New life-styles and diversified consumer tastes are emerging, and these could provide greater opportunities for EC exporters. The post-war consumption revolution in Western countries, initially brought about by major socio-economic changes, was matched by greater spending power, and in recent years the arrival of socially mobile young professionals has opened up more specialist markets for goods like clothing and consumer durables. Through foreign travel and exposure to Western culture, Japanese youth has followed these trends; it could be said that ever since their country began to modernise in the late nineteenth century, no people has been as keen as the Japanese to adopt Western ways and fashions—always providing, however, that these are not too much at variance with their traditional culture. In recent years greater affluence among the young has created several small specialist markets for Western goods— witness the success of BMW cars in the mid-1980's, an example which other European manufacturers could well try to emulate. However, in spite of the emergence of this type of clientele, EC exporters have found it difficult to penetrate Japan's complex distribution systems. The Japanese prefer to take their time developing business relationships, long-term market share being more important to them than immediate profit; with their different attitudes, foreigners do not immediately fit easily into this milieu. Moreover, distribution involving many middlemen favours domestic suppliers at the expense of EC exporters. It has proved time consuming and expensive for Europeans to establish and staff their own distribution systems in Japan when individual Japanese companies dominated and controlled market outlets. Ever responsive to changes in style and fashion, the Japanese are keen buyers of expensive high-quality British luxury goods like cashmere sweaters, but in everyday purchases they show great loyalty to local brands. As of the early 1980s, for instance, 75 per cent of outlets for electrical goods were tied to particular Japanese firms. For their part, the Japanese have in recent years started to get rid of tariff and non-tariff barriers; the onus is now on EC exporters to develop better marketing strategies, especially through co-operation with local Japanese firms in direct retailing so that foreign products can become household names.

The Japanese accuse EC businessmen of too little marketing effort, so few of them taking the trouble to learn about Japan's language and culture. There have, however, been some foreign success stories, a case in point being the British firm, Gunson's Sortex, which makes sorting machines for agricultural produce. It came onto the Japanese scene twenty five years ago and has been the exception to the rule, conducting research and taking advantage of economic change. When Japanese rice prices were government controlled, there was no incentive for producers to introduce a sorting process but when, in the late 1960s, a semi-free market was established, Sortex had a field free of rivals.[11] The company engaged the Marubeni Corporation, a large Japanese trading house, to handle sales, import documentation and port clearances, and has since gained between 5 and 10 per cent of the market. Typically Japanese tactics have been followed, emphasising low production costs and low profit margins.[12]

The same logic could be applied to selling consumer goods, and new trends in Japan's retail distribution systems could offer greater opportunity to EC exporters. Much retail selling in Japan has ben governed in the post-war years by the shopping habits of Japanese housewives who, lacking storage space in their small homes, shop for food on a day-to-day basis, thus supporting a large number of small local shops (usually family-run). In the grocery and other sectors of the retail trade, rationalisation has been impeded by the Big Stores Law, legislation making the construction of supermarkets and department stores subject to approval by local shopkeepers. In spite of this, however, the traditional retail structure has been changing, with increased affluence leading to a demand for a greater range of merchandise, and not only in food. In addition, as more women enter the work-force and better housing provides more storage space, daily purchases will give way to bulk buying.[13] Already self-service chainstores (offering lower prices) as well as specialty stores have grown rapidly in the last two decades, to some extent at the expense of neighbourhood shops. Department stores, some names dating back over a century, have enhanced their competitiveness by stocking foreign goods, and they are in a good position to promote Western brand names in fields like fashion apparel, household goods and food items. Furthermore, the trend towards greater concentration of ownership in the Japanese retail sector favours importers, and in turn EC exporters, who can gain more business either through direct dealing or via trading companies. Even small neighbourhood stores have organised themselves into associations to retain their share of the market, thus offering further scope for specialist imports. Yet most of the initiatives to date have come from Japanese retailers and trading companies, and EC exporters must adopt a more aggressive approach if they are to increase their share of the Japanese market.[14]

Modern technology offers other ways of conquering Japan's distribution system. In January 1987 American goods went on sale in Japan via a television satellite link-up, the orders being sent by express mail direct from the USA. One consequence of this has been to make Japanese consumers more aware of the higher prices usually charged for a whole range of EC luxury goods—sometimes up to three times their price in Western Europe.[15]

The full impact of these social trends and changes will be felt only in the long term, and the correction of EC-Japan trade imbalances will be a slow process. In the light of protectionist calls against the onslaught of Japanese goods in EC countries and the US demand that the Japanese pull their weight in the Western alliance, some observers have proposed that Japan should become a major arms manufacturer so as to reduce its trade surpluses. In fact, shortly after the Japanese 1987 budget which breached the one per cent limit on defence spending, US spokesmen publicly suggested a role for Japan in improving NATO's weapons technology as part of the Conventional Defence Initiative.[16] Any such defence arrangements could also be reciprocal; the British Tornado, for example, might yet serve as a strike fighter in the Japanese Air Self-Defence Force. The beginning of the next Defence Build-Up Plan in 1991 could mean significant procurements at home and abroad.

In summary, fundamental economic and social changes in Japan could help to redress trade surpluses but the nature of the EC-Japan relationship is increasingly being conditioned by a world of economic interdependence; the various aspects of co-operation between the two sides are dealt with in the next chapter.

5

Japan-EC Relations: Economic Co-operation and Conflict Resolution?

It has become the conventional wisdom among Western observers to claim that Japan's rise to the position of the world's second economic power has been achieved through a unique social dynamic but at great social cost, as exemplified by poor public amenities like inferior housing and urban overcrowding. Certainly, factors such as social discipline and the subordination of the individual to the group have helped to boost Japan's national income while the standard of living of ordinary Japanese is only just beginning to approach that of their EC counterparts; but there is a sense in which arguments of this kind have been accepted on trust and economic arguments not sufficiently taken into account.

Recent Western studies, however, have re-examined the idea of Japanese uniqueness which was originally fostered by Japan's nineteenth-century modernisers to achieve national unity. In the face of encroachment by the West, the Japanese genius was to revive and reactivate the traditions that had fallen into abeyance; the position of the Emperor was enhanced and exalted as a focus of national unity just as the ancient idea of the divine origin of the Japanese people was resuscitated and incorporated in the new concept of the nation. Similarly, the adoption of foreign technologies and institutions was a means to an end, and whenever possible they were given a Japanese cast: the country's leaders sought national survival and prosperity by competing in a Western-dominated system of international relations, but it was not to gain understanding of and empathy with foreign countries for their own sake. In fact, so successful were Japan's modernisers in cultivating the idea of uniqueness or *Nihonjinron*—the theory of the Japanese—that even Westerners came to believe the Japanese argument, and Japan's search for and success in obtaining raw material supplies were not matched by full and

104

proper knowledge of Japan's economy and society on the part of Westerners. To them Japan seemed different; it was an advanced industrial country but indisputably Oriental and not subject to European laws of social and economic development.[1]

In the late 1980s Japan's economic advance was undiminished and earlier trends confirmed as the Japanese weathered the recession better than their trading partners. By 1986 Japan's world trade surplus had reached a record US$83 billion, the largest of any one country—and it was only a little lower at almost US$80 billion in 1987—while the EC's trade deficit with Japan reached an all-time high of US$18 billion in 1986.[2] This outcome was reflected in Japan's trade with individual EC countries; British exports to Japan, for example, accounted for less than a third of imports into Britain from Japan in 1987.[3] The health of the Japanese economy *vis-à-vis* its competitors continued to be underlined by a low rate of inflation, averaging just 0.1 per cent in 1987, and an unemployment rate of under 3 per cent (even through unemployment is measured differently in Japan from Western countries).[4]

By early 1988 it was apparent that the 1985 measure revaluing the yen had only been partially successful in improving the export competitiveness of Western countries, and EC complaints against unfair Japanese trading practices persisted (although the countries of the Community varied in their reaction, say, to imports of Japanese cars). As inveterate free traders, the Germans maintained an open car market, of which the Japanese share was almost 15 per cent in 1986, a situation seen as favourable by German manufacturers who were having more success than others in selling to Japan. In contrast, the French limited the Japanese to 3 per cent of their own car market, the equivalent figure for Japan's sales in Britain being about 10 per cent. But while Japanese car sales in Europe are still largely concentrated at the popular end of the market, the enormous rise in the value of the yen against the US dollar in 1986 gave an advantage to European exporters—particularly in specialist areas like the luxury car market, enhancing prospects for Austin Rover, Volkswagen, BMW and Mercedes—as European unit costs fell below those in Japan. For instance, BMW's total sales of 1,600 cars in Japan in 1975 increased to 15,000 in 1986.[5] It is these specialist areas that the EC should target. In fact, it is of mutual advantage to industrial countries like the countries of the EC and Japan to engage in 'horizontal trade' of this kind. Such trade is, however, partially dependent on lifting more trade barriers. While the EC is by no means blameless in this regard, the Japanese—in spite of having lowered many import duties—still protect their domestic producers, some of the most notorious examples being in the food and drink sectors. Take, for instance, the liquor lobby in Japan which has so long prevented successive Japanese governments from reducing discriminatory taxes on Scotch whisky and other imported alcoholic drinks. In addition, horizontal trade can only be successful if nations concentrate on those economic sectors to which they are best suited by virtue of their skills and natural endowments.

Measures to reduce friction with the EC and promote horizontal trade were reflected in the Japanese government's three-year 'Action Programme for Improved Market Access', adopted in July 1985. By July 1987 tariffs had been eliminated or reduced on the 2,000 or so items listed in the programme, and this resulted in increased government purchases of foreign products. Positive steps were also taken to encourage major corporations to purchase overseas goods; witness the activities of the Japan External Trade Organisation (JETRO), a government body which, since 1982, has established information bureaux for exporters in major EC cities, and officially sponsored import fairs for department stores and retail chains in various parts of Japan. To be noted also are the Export-Import Bank's measures to lower interest rates and extend loan periods to facilitate the importation of manufactured goods.

Ultimately, however, voluntary quotas on Japanese exports, the lowering of tariffs and a higher yen exchange rate are but palliatives in a world of increasing economic interdependence. Co-operation must be based on mutual understanding, a long-term, two-way process requiring patient negotiation and more cultural links of one kind and another.

A significant move in this direction was the formation in 1984 of the 2000 Group, financed from both official and private sources, designed as a forum for reconciling British and Japanese differences and made up of politicians, businessmen and academics. It has a counterpart Japanese body. The 2000 Group's brief, however, was much broader than the resolution of Anglo-Japanese trade frictions, expressing as it did support for free trade under GATT, the need for closer international co-operation, and a call for capital and technical assistance to developing countries. Though concerned with only one country in the EC and possibly suspect in the eyes of other members, the 200 Group's consultations have helped to define areas of economic co-operation by focusing on the new technologies and their impact on manufacturing processes, the provision of education for innovation and retraining as well as their effects on employment and social structures. In similar vein, in early 1988 the British Foreign Secretary, Sir Geoffrey Howe, and his Japanese opposite number, Mr Sosuke Uno, agreed to annual contacts at the level of minister and permanent secretary and to encourage non-governmental exchanges within the business, parliamentary and youth communities:[6] the objective is to lay the foundation for long-term industrial collaboration and joint ventures in Britain, Japan and other countries. Increasingly, too, there is recognition by the Japanese themselves that they are no longer followers but leaders, second only perhaps to the United States, and therefore they should take on greater responsibility to help cure the world's economic and financial ills. Moves to date towards economic co-operation must, however, be seen against the background of Japanese measures to restructure their own economy during the late 1980s. One aspect of current Japanese government economic policy has been to further trends already in motion as a result of the high yen exchange rate and earlier adjustments to changes in world markets.

Yen revaluation in 1985 had been intended to reduce Japanese exports to the EC and the United States by making them more expensive and less competitive *vis-à-vis* foreign goods and simultaneously to facilitate the entry of cheaper overseas manufactures into Japan. As in the past, however, such as during the oil crises of the 1970s, the Japanese have shown a healthy instinct for their own survival. In any case the prices of imported raw materials like oil have fallen in the late 1980s, thus keeping Japanese manufacturing costs within bounds. Clearly, too, rationalisation in industry through increased automation and robotisation, reductions in executive salaries, moves out of older and less efficient industries and the initiation of offshore production have played their part in the adjustment to a higher yen. The resilience of the Japanese economy also enabled Japan to avoid the more devastating effects of the October 1987 'black Monday' crash, with equity falls being only about half those in Britain and the United States—though also important were institutional factors like the close relationship between government and big business, types of government controls over the Stock Exchange and the nature of shareholding distribution.

Developments towards international economic interdependence are not, however, proving entirely painless for Japan, and

Japanese government measures have been initiated to effect a smoother transition and to contain adverse social effects at home. Conscious of the need for good public relations, in 1985 Prime Minister Nakasone unveiled (through the Maekawa Committee) a plan for the comprehensive restructuring of Japan's economy. The Maekawa Report (1986) outlined various objectives, the most immediate and crucial of which was the need to reduce Japan's current account surplus through the expansion of domestic demand for foreign goods. Japan could be a huge market for foreign exporters, especially EC manufacturers, but before its full potential can be realised certain conditions must be met.

A popular image of Japan has hitherto been of a nation importing minerals and energy while selling manufactured goods abroad, and yet most of Japan's products are sold on the domestic market; only 17 per cent of Japan's domestic output is exported, a figure lower than the equivalent for other major industrial countries.[7] Nevertheless Japan has a high cost of living, and rigidities in the price structure are preventing the advantages of a strong yen reaching the Japanese public. Some observers have suggested that Japan's exporters have coped with the yen revaluation by raising the prices of manufactures at home, thus offsetting losses on exports.[8]

More fundamental to foreign exporters seeking to exploit market potential in Japan are financial and cultural factors. Because of the need for frugality to rebuild Japan's economy after World War II, there has been a high propensity to save in Japan, itself encouraged by the tax system. In 1987 attempts at tax reform were stymied by vested interests and political complications, but by early 1988 one important measure—that abolishing the Maruyu system exempting small savers from taxation and subject to serious abuse through multiple accounts—was already in process, with a new levy of 20 per cent on deposits of 3 million yen (about £13,260 at the rate of exchange then current). Also planned were income and corporate tax cuts, to be replaced by sales taxes, designed to stimulate Japan's economy, increase imports and boost direct overseas investment. Tax reform is thus also intended to reduce Japan's growing internal deficit.

It has often been remarked by foreign observers that while Japan's national income has increased rapidly, standards of public amenities and welfare benefits have lagged far behind. One reason for the high rate of personal saving in the post-war period has been the belated and slow development of state-sponsored welfare and pension systems. Though large companies have provided for their own employees in these matters, some sectors of the population have been less fortunate and in 1987, following the recommendations of the Maekawa Report, the government turned its attention to increasing social capital. It was mooted that part of the earnings from the sale of the publicly-owned Nippon Telegraph and Telephone Corporation stock to private investors would be transferred to a special industrial investment account for improving public amenities.

Housing construction and public works like road projects are being given priority by government but a substantial role is envisaged for the private sector and local government. To help in the development of private residential property, the government's Housing Loan Corporation announced the provision of 700 billion yen in additional finance for the construction of new houses; but one barrier to the creation of better and cheaper housing has been the shortage of land near major cities like Tokyo, partially a by-product of the American Occupation's land reform and subsequent legislation. In addition, as a result of high rice subsidies, farmers have no incentive to put land up for sale and only in recent years have governments shown signs of daring to go against the wishes of a powerful agricultural lobby. Yet the demands of economic restructuring seem likely to galvanise successive Japanese administrations into action on this and other pressing issues, as only through increasing the availability of residential land is further investment in housing possible.

Enhancing living standards is dependent on continued wealth creation and the Japanese have shown considerable capacity for adapting to world economic trends. By early 1987 Japan's unemployment rate was the highest since records began in 1959, a contributing factor being the decline of industries like steel and shipbuilding and this trend was in evidence before the revaluation of the yen. Spin-off effects have included less demand for coal and more unemployment among workers in small subcontracting firms who produce for major companies but are not on their regular payroll. Retraining staff of large firms and initiating voluntary retirement schemes are only a partial answer, and in any case do not apply to temporary workers.

To survive in an increasingly competitive world Japan's major steelmakers announced in 1987 rationalisation plans designed to reduce their combined work-force by 40,000, about 30 per cent of the total, between 1988 and 1990. Companies in other industries have sought to cut costs by undertaking work previously done by sub-contractors.

The long-term solution, however, lies in the establishment of new high-technology industries because rapidly developing Asian countries like South Korea and Taiwan have moved into traditional areas of Japanese competence like 'smokestack' industries.[9]

In Western writing much weight has been given to the close links between business and government, a relationship which is much more structured than in other advanced industrial countries. As discussed earlier, the Japanese have been moving away from subsidies and import barriers as tools of industrial policy, and the Japanese Cabinet's business voice, the Ministry of International Trade and Industry, now emphasises knowledge-gathering and the dissemination of information on industrial restructuring. A case in point is MITI's recent emphasis on knowledge-intensive industries, a priority addressed through the Ministry and the Industrial Structure Council, composed of industrialists, academics, former officials and journalists. MITI organised private forums for research into very large-scale integration (VLSI), laser-beam technology, computer software capability and fifth generation computers.[10]

Moreover, as Japanese industry moves into the new technologies, a greater premium is being placed on the role of the innovative entrepreneur; the old emphasis on mass production of identical consumer goods will give way, in the words of JETRO, to more diversified small-lot production. These trends are especially evident in the small- and medium-sized enterprises for which special government loan facilities have been arranged. In addition, as the prospect of increased unemployment has loomed, the government has taken measures to provide work for 300,000 people under the Employment Development Programme as well as introducing vocational training schemes similar to those in other advanced industrial countries.

Simultaneously, in 1987, measures were planned to promote local industries that take full advantage of local strengths and resources. Thus domestic demand is being promoted through more foreign imports and industrial restructuring, capital investment in private sector research and development as well as greater provision of loan services by financial institutions.[11]

Increased domestic demand means higher living standards and a better quality of life. The shortfall in social amenities has already been commented on; increased leisure makes the extension of these that much more crucial. In summary, such objectives as more housing and improved social capital are being given higher priority. The desire of the EC countries is to expand their exports to Japan but by late 1987 the Japanese were heading for another record trade surplus with the rest of the world.

As of 1988, Japanese ventures and investment in the EC were far more extensive than those of the EC states in Japan, and the same is true of capital markets. With this in mind, attention will first be focused on Japanese economic co-operation in EC countries.

Just as EC countries have failed to present a united front in the face of Japanese trade surpluses, so also do they lack consensus on the desirability and optimal conditions for Japanese-led joint ventures and investment in the Community. But in acknowledging the growing interdependence of the world's major economies, individual EC countries and Japan see that it is to their mutual advantage to foster joint ventures and exchange technological expertise. Their strengths in some sectors may be made even greater and weaknesses in others made good.

As early as the late 1970s there were discussions at Community level as to how economic co-operation with Japan might benefit the EC—witness the Senior Commission Officials Report of 1979. A wider perspective was emerging, and talks on trade issues were extended to industrial co-operation, facilitating arrangements which would not have emerged from a purely surplus/deficit perspective.[12] One outcome was the formation in 1982 of the EC-Japan Centre for Industrial Co-operation, designed to train European businessmen in Japanese methods and, more importantly, to promote bilateral investments, with a jointly-funded budget.[13]

What were the motives of the two parties? Japan's wealth is increasingly being channelled into investments abroad, making the country the world's biggest exporter of capital. The Japanese are thereby creating riches for themselves no longer obtainable by the old method of territorial conquest. (It should also be remembered in this context, however, that the British have transferred oil wealth into a diversified portfolio of foreign assets, helping to make Britain the second wealthiest nation after Japan in terms of the ownership of foreign assets.)[14] Japanese investments in the EC so far have been considerably lower than those in the United States but the rationale is the same: on the one

hand, there is self-interest since the revalued yen has made production costs more economic in those countries than Japan; on
the other hand, production in other countries is a means of
warding off threats of protectionism against Japan's export surpluses and as well, direct investment in foreign industries creates
jobs and assists industrial restructuring. Indeed, there is competition among EC countries for Japanese investment. Envious of
Britain's success in attracting Japanese investment, countries like
France, the Netherlands, and West Germany are trying to attract
Japanese companies, and they have had some success: in 1987
Volkswagen of the Federal German Republic and Toyota Motor
Corporation agreed to co-operate in producing 15,000 Toyota
pick-up trucks a year at Volkswagen's Hannover plant.[15] A possible long-term solution is an agreed division of labour both within
and between countries although this should never be allowed
to rule out a healthy spirit of competition.

Debates in the European Parliament have reflected this resentment over the bulk of Japanese investment and ventures being
concentrated in Britain and, to a lesser extent, West Germany.
Calls for a unified Community policy on the motor industry,
for example, imply that the rest of the EC countries are at an
unfair disadvantage in the short term, and yet there is a sense
in which investment crossing national boundaries is shifting competition from nations to corporate groupings.[16]

There is no doubt that for language reasons—English becoming universal—and because the United Kingdom is a lead market
for, say, consumer electronic goods, the Japanese have targeted
Britain as their main field of investment. The late 1980s have
seen an acceleration of Japanese investment in new factories and
other facilities, with a rise of about 30 per cent in the 1986–87
financial year bringing the value of the Japanese stake in Britain
to a little over US$4 billion. (The percentage increase in the
previous year was only 13.5 per cent). By early 1988 there were
over seventy manufacturing companies established in Britain,
ranging from YKK Zip Fasteners (1972) to the Nissan car factory
in North-east England (1986). Another key sector is electronics,
an example being Brother Industries in South Wales, established
(like several other Japanese ventures) in a depressed area and
thus providing new employment opportunities, though on a relatively small scale.[17] Japanese investment is creating its own
momentum, and further developments projected by JVC in
Scotland's Silicon Glen will benefit from a good business environment and a skilled labour force as well as from the presence

of existing Japanese companies and Scotland's increasing prominence as a business centre.

Events have moved rapidly for the electronics world since Sony—the most prominent Japanese investor in the European consumer field with plants in the United Kingdom, France, West Germany and Spain–opened a colour television factory in South Wales in 1974. Sony was followed in rapid succession by Matsushita, Hitachi, Mitsubishi, Aiwa, Toshiba, Sanyo, Sharp and Brother. Other companies investing in Britain in the light engineering field include Yamazaki, a machine tools manufacturer, and Komatsu, a leading manufacturer of construction equipment.[18]

Like national governments, other European car and electronics manufacturers have complained about the alleged unfair competition resulting from Japanese investment which is also seen as a means of avoiding EC tariffs—the Trojan horse syndrome. Certainly, in the late 1970s Japanese factories in Britain did begin as 'screwdriver operations', assembling products from Japanese-made kits with little local content, and as these were regarded as imports for tariff purposes, they partly defeated the object of Japanese investment. But in the 1980s local content increased with the inputs of British components. Most Japanese manufacturers are aiming to increase the local content above 50 per cent (60 per cent in the case of cars, as of 1988) at which point products are deemed to be of European origin. Of course, British component suppliers create employment; suppliers for Nissan include Triplex for glass, Firth for carpets and Dunlop for tyres, among others. The Nissan Bluebird cars produced at the company's plant at Washington in North-east England escape the import quota on Japanese cars—the voluntary agreement to keep imports down to 11 per cent of the British car market. As of 1988 most of the cars from the Nissan plant were to be sold in the United Kingdom. Nissan imports already took 5.7 per cent of the British market in 1988.[19] (Organisations like Nissan are still subsidiaries of Japanese companies with overseas factories rather than true multinationals with autonomous companies in different countries).

In this way the Japanese protect their markets while EC countries gain employment as well as the skills created by technological improvements demanded of component suppliers by Japanese manufacturers. It is through their technological lead in key industries that the Japanese have reached and held on to their international economic position. Both sides benefit by the substitution of local EC production for Japanese imports but Europe will not benefit in the long term if Japanese manufacturers penetrate new markets formerly the preserve of Western companies. There is no certainty that Japanese firms will limit production and sales to markets they already possess.

While the Japanese have invested abroad, there are sectors in which Europeans remain pre-eminent, and future co-operation in EC countries will not be a one-way process. Seeing the long-term advantages of technological co-operation, a 1982 MITI White Paper envisaged greater interchange with the West. While the Japanese had often excelled in the application of new technology, their weaknesses in pure science could be put right by collaboration with EC countries which in return would have greater access to the latest Japanese practical skills. While the Japanese in the past have dominated the lower end of the mass markets—in electronic consumer goods, for example,—there is less certainty that they will maintain their superiority as that sector merges with those of computers and telecommunications: thus, Japanese computer hardware has not always been accompanied by adequate software. Future joint ventures will depend on the willingness to share information. Collaboration may be envisaged in different ways: to Europeans it often means joint ventures and licensing agreements while the Japanese have often thought in terms of 100 per cent direct investment and thus, in the view of some Europeans, control.[20]

Japanese investment has brought in its train aspects of Japanese management practice, though there are already signs of two-way influences, as in the field of industrial relations. Japanese economic success has often been partly attributed to smooth labour relations, held up as a model by Western admirers. Solidarity within Japanese enterprises is seen to derive from organisation and a task-oriented workforce; employees aim to excel in the area they have been allotted and seek to sharpen their company's competitive edge. In contrast, Western workers and managers, so the argument goes, have a stronger sense of identity with their trade or profession than their firm.[21] Although by the late 1980s Japanese companies like Hitachi and Nissan were sending young managers to European business schools, other Japanese graduates of similar Western institutions are still often channelled into the less traditional international divisions of Japanese companies. This secondment of Japanese managers has served a reconnaissance purpose for the firms concerned; whether it will further Japanese understanding of or sympathy for Western management practices is less clear.[22]

Even though it would be fanciful to imagine that practices can be easily transplanted from one society to another, the Japanese can claim some success in adapting features of their industrial relations to their ventures in Britain. Some observers believe that British workers have been quite willing to accept some Japanese methods; thus although the Japanese seniority system (on which promotion is based), has been generally unacceptable to the British, the willingness of Japanese companies to keep workers informed of future developments as well as the greater accountability of management have earned high praise—as too have product quality, job security and in-house training schemes.

Perhaps the greatest reservations have been expressed by British managers in Japan's enterprises in Britain; they fear that consultation with workers in line with Japanese practices will undermine their authority, reducing their decision-making powers, and thus make them less marketable when they apply for management positions elsewhere.[23] In addition, the British side of management has often claimed that they are denied the rapport which their Japanese colleagues have with their headquarters in Tokyo. On balance, then, the greatest Japanese public relations successes have been achieved *vis-à-vis* the workforce as opposed to management—though Japanese enterprises in Britain have not been immune from industrial action, as witnessed the pay dispute at the zip company's YKK's factory at Runcorn in 1985.

Through the exchange and secondment of both managers and workforce, Japanese investment will have an impact not only on labour relations but on technical standards in EC industries. By the same token, given European technological strengths, there are strong arguments in favour of EC-led joint ventures in Japan itself; while the Japanese seek to retain European markets through judicious investment, it is in the interest of EC manufacturers to do the same in Japan. Indeed, a major objective of the Maekawa Report is the encouragement of foreign investment in Japan. In the early post-war years tight restrictions prevented foreign investors gaining control of Japanese companies but in May 1973 the government accepted the principle of 100 per cent direct foreign investment in new or existing Japanese firms, but this has been slow to materialise. As with trade the greatest investment potential lies in specialist sectors and high-technology industries. But in early 1988 Prime Minister Noboru Takeshita—no doubt mindful of his country's reliance on the United States for both defence and raw materials—was proving more responsive to American than EC appeals for investment access to Japan's economy. A case in point was the proposal he made in Washington to allow American companies to participate, on a preferential basis, in large public-works projects including port and airport expansion, a concession which predictably brought a stern reaction from European leaders who condemned such bilateral arrangements as contravening GATT.[24]

But while, at the time of writing, EC investments in Japan have not been as extensive as those of their Japanese counterparts in Europe, there have been some notable EC successes in recent years, mainly in the production of high quality goods at the upper end of specialist markets, and by the 1980s there were over a thousand Europe-related companies in Japan. In April 1983, British Leyland's Austin Rover Group and Japan's Honda contracted to produce British and Japanese versions of a new executive car in both countries, and later Austin Rover Japan was to become a wholly-owned unit of the Rover Group.

Much investment, however, has been concentrated in chemical and pharmaceutical fields represented by companies like Hoechst, ICI and Beechams. An instance of a specialist undertaking may be cited. In December 1983 Oxford Instruments—a firm making magnets used in new body scanners which have made X-ray medical diagnoses obsolete—announced a joint venture with Furukawa Electric, and leading companies like Toshiba and Hitachi contracted to sell the products in Japan. In a highly competitive technological field, manufacture in Japan gives such companies a head start over potential rivals in capturing crucial markets in the Far East and the USA. More importantly, the presence of European firms, whether in the form of subsidiaries or joint ventures, does cultivate Japanese taste and demand for European goods and services. One factor favouring the Westernisation of Japanese consumer taste is the start of the five-day week in Japan. By 1984, a JETRO source claims, 35 per cent of all Japanese workers were regularly having two days off work a week. There will thus be greater recreational opportunities and increased leisure spending. The Japanese Diet in 1987 accepted the principle of a work week of forty six hours or less (a forty-hour week being the norm in most Western industrial countries).[25] Those trends could well increase the profits of EC luxury goods subsidiaries or joint ventures in Japan.

As stated earlier on, foreign observers have singled out cultural factors as major barriers to the Japanese market, especially as manifested in the exclusive and complex distribution systems of Japan. Apart from stories about Japanese bad faith, there is no doubt that Japanese ways of decision-making and negotiating contracts must be taken into account by joint venture partners from the EC. Encouragingly, the Japanese Business Services Unit at Sheffield University, established in 1983, offers Japanese language and cultural courses to personnel from firms with plans for trade and joint ventures with Japan.

The decision-making process in Japan often appears slow and cumbersome but this reflects in part the long view, as the Japanese value continuity in business relationships more than do the Europeans. Thus while the Japanese sign and honour agreements, they are not a litigious people and business relationships are more personalised than contractual; great importance is attached to maintaining 'face' in Japan and '*honne*', roughly translated as true or actual intentions—may not be immediately revealed. ('*Honne*' is to be distinguished from '*tatemae*' which is merely the front presented). Confidence between partners has to be built up over a period of time, and so Western-style straightforward negotiation is often likely to hinder any early progress. In addition, because of the premium placed on consensus in Japanese enterprises, top-level discussion can only be successful if numbers of lower and middle-level personnel are consulted. Similarly, foreign companies need to be in contact with top executives and middle-management promoters within the Japanese company over their proposals and discuss with those who put the proposals into effect. The advantages of this procedure from the Japanese side are that several executives study proposals from many different angles, each one thereby having a stake in the final decision and the venture's success.

Recognising this process of '*nemawashi*'—laying the groundwork—is crucial if EC-Japan economic co-operation is to be achieved. Initially, the Japanese favour general agreements initialled by both parties rather than a detailed and lengthy Western-style legal contract—since this, to the Japanese identifies the foreign side as adversaries and not as partners. In Japan the initial written agreement is a declaration of intent, dealing with specifics only where describing the technology or services which the foreign company is expected to provide. This practice springs from the informal nature of obligations stemming from the homogeneity of Japanese society but it does also provide flexibility should external circumstances change and has often been used to advantage by Japanese negotiators.

Goodwill through human relationships rather than signed contracts together with harmonious consultation as opposed to arbitration clauses—these are the watchwords of successful co-operation according to the Japanese. They provide an insight into the conduct of Japanese companies which are willing to do business—even without profit in the short term—in the belief that they will benefit in the long run.

Foreign partners fail to recognise these features of Japanese business at their peril. This is not to say, however, that the Japanese themselves are not impatient to acquire the most up-to-date Western technology through joint ventures, and EC partners must take steps to ensure, especially through work-force practices, that they make substantial long-term gains from their subsidiaries and investments in Japan.[26]

Different approaches to management-labour relations have conditioned EC and Japanese attitudes to the use of both human and technological resources. Some writers have seen the small number of successful Western-Japanese joint ventures as due to European or American failure to consider the management of human resources as a means to hold competitive advantage derived, say, from superior technology; instead the West has relied excessively on equity ownership or legal methods to limit the Japanese partners' initiative. This is a different issue from that of Japanese consensus decision-making but it does point to the Westerners' neglect of the human factor. Thus, EC and American partners have often not built management teams independent of their Japanese counterparts and recruitment and training have been dominated by the Japanese firms. As a result it has been difficult for EC and other Western companies to win the loyalty and commitment of their Japanese employees; the independent identity of the joint venture has not been sufficiently emphasised. For the European companies a major purpose of co-operation is consequently defeated, as they gain little knowledge of the Japanese market.[27]

The arguments of those who claim that the Japanese are interested in making good certain weaknesses in their technology but not in genuine partnership with foreigners is thus reinforced, but the fault lies also with Westerners themselves.

Given a spirit of goodwill and co-operation on both sides, none of these problems is insurmountable. Once again, however, just as in the case of foreign investment in industrial enterprises, the Japanese have so far been more active and successful in EC capital and services markets than their European counterparts have in Japan. Similarly, too, while the Japanese have been slow to liberalise their financial institutions, the onus is again on EC countries to prove the competitiveness of the services they have to offer.

Japanese activity in foreign capital and stock markets is looked at next. The realignment of exchange rates in 1985 by the major powers—the USA, Japan, Britain, France and West Germany—had the intended result of boosting the value of the yen, making Japanese exports less competitive (though Japanese trade surpluses, especially with the EC and the USA, actually rose in 1988). To a large extent this realignment, as stated above, accelerated trends that were already in being in Japan where there were moves into new industries. There was renewed interest, particularly on the part of export-dependent manufactures, in the stock market at home and overseas where they hoped to recoup some of the losses they were incurring to maintain market shares abroad.[28] Moreover, because of a high level of corporate liquidity in Japan and decreased loan demand, certain Japanese banks have found their local market unattractive, and they have turned to overseas markets where there is less regulation than in Japan, both to make profits and to learn new banking skills in readiness for financial liberalisation in Tokyo. Finally, in view of interest rate cuts and changes in post office account rules, in 1988 the Japanese were turning away from banks and moving into stocks and shares.

These developments, have made Japan a major exporter of capital on a par with Saudi Arabia at the time of the 1970s oil boom. While traditionally a good deal of Japanese overseas investment has been placed in American treasury bills—helping to finance US budget deficits—the Japanese have been diversifying in their search for higher yields, channelling money into London where Japan's presence now parallels her growing manufacturing base in Britain.[29] Japanese commercial banks have traditionally followed their domestic clients abroad.

Like their manufacturing counterparts, Japanese banks and securities houses have been accused of unfair practices in establishing themselves in foreign markets, their chief tactic being to sacrifice short-term profits for long-term gain. Japanese banks too are more prominent in London than British institutions in Tokyo, suggesting that financial liberalisation in Japan is far from complete.

There is no doubt that Japanese banks have been fulfilling a need by lending to British local authorities and companies at competitive rates. To date, the Japanese banks' main focus has been wholesale financial markets and they have yet to penetrate the retail sectors, the branches in Britain's high streets.

The Japanese genius has been to take advantage of buoyant or new markets, and the growing Eurobond and Euronote markets based in London are no exception to that rule. These bonds and notes are replacing commercial lending as the main form of international financing. As financial liberalisation has proceeded in Japan, albeit slowly, Japanese funds can be moved overseas more easily and have been placed in currencies such as US dollars, deutschmarks or sterling—or increasingly as it appreciates in value, their own yen. These instruments are underwritten by banks and securities houses which provide borrowers with funds through selling the bonds and notes to their clients. As these bonds and notes can be changed from one currency into another, buyers may profit from movements in exchange or interest rates; thus the increasing attraction to investors of bonds denominated in yen and underwritten by the big four Japanese securities houses of Nomura, Daiwa, Nikko and Yamaichi—all of which have been playing a major role in new Euromarket issues via their London branches. Significantly, Euroyen securities are being issued by both European and Japanese borrowers, and Japanese have travelled to London to buy because it has been cheaper to borrow yen outside Japan. For Japanese banks, issuing bonds has also been a reconnaissance operation, as under the provisions of Article 65 of the Japanese Securities Act (modelled on the American Glass Steagall Act) they have in the past been barred from dealing in securities (although through the establishment of investment companies this barrier has been surmounted, and famous names such as Sumitomo, Mitsubishi, Dai-Ichi and the Industrial Bank of Japan have featured prominently in bond dealing). The banks are thus acquiring the skills necessary when revision of Article 65 permits them to enter the securities business in Japan itself.[30]

Since the mid-1950s individual Japanese investors have followed manufacturers, banks and securities houses in showing increased interest in foreign financial instruments, especially equities. Securities houses have been helping the Japanese to diversify their portfolios, and institutions like Nomura (which became a member of the London Stock Exchange in March 1986) have stepped up their research into the activities of British companies in time-honoured Japanese fashion and thoroughness by recruiting specialists from the City of London and British universities.

Finally, the high propensity of Japanese to save for private insurance and pension funds has contributed to Japan's role in foreign capital markets. In the spring of 1987 Japan's Ministry of Finance permitted Japanese life insurance companies, awash with pension funds, to increase the proportion they could hold in overseas securities from 10 per cent to 30 per cent of their assets.[31] Already over twenty Japanese insurance firms operate in the City of London, and in 1988 one of Japan's largest, Sumitomo, took a substantial stake in Ivory and Sime, the Edinburgh-based investment management company; the linkage between the latter's international investment experience and Japan's high level of personal savings was seen as benefiting both parties.[32]

Japanese banks, securities houses and insurance companies are not only increasing the wealth of their own clients but creating jobs and bringing funds into Britain. In any case the Japanese presence is two-edged; in addition to selling Japanese shares to British clients like insurance companies, Japan's securities houses have also been active in selling European stocks to Japanese. Nomura, for example, sold 100 million British Telecom shares to 40,000 investors in Japan.[33] For Britain and other EC countries to retaliate because the Japanese commodity and capital markets are being liberalised too slowly would be counterproductive in the long run; economic interdependence demands horizontal trade, the exploitation of individual strengths and the close monitoring of economic agreements.   Deregulation of Japan's financial institutions and markets has been under way since the mid-1970s although their services have been and still remain more protected than Japan's consumer goods industries. Deregulation may be examined within the following framework: the liberalisation of Japan's money and capital markets through the relaxation of interest rate controls, the expansion of domestic money markets and the easier access of foreign institutions to Japanese financial bodies like the Tokyo Stock Exchange. Specific reforms in these areas began as early as 1976 and have since been designed to enhance the role of market forces by relaxing interest rate constraints and increasing portfolio opportunities for market participants; securities markets are being further developed for both private and public debt. Capital flows to and from Japan have been eased through the 1980 amendment to the Foreign Exchange and Foreign Trade Control Law.[34]

Just as industry is helped along into innovation and new technologies by employer-government committees, so also do governments in Japan nurture and protect the financial sector. In the wake of deregulation, however, this pattern has been slowly changing in relation to the banks, the securities houses and the Tokyo Stock Exchange. From the early post-war years until the 1970s the Ministry of Finance clearly defined the roles of long-term credit and trust banks, and foreign participation was strictly controlled. But by 1980 the Japanese financial institutions were strong enough to compete internationally and most exchange controls were lifted. Banking has thus become more subject to competition both from home and abroad and foreign banks, like Barclays in 1985, have been admitted to the trust banking business in Japan. There are other challenges too; although Japan's domestic banks reign supreme in granting certain kinds of loan, securities are playing an increasing role in finance and here foreign banks enjoy special privileges denied to their Japanese equivalents. Nevertheless, in spite of these advantages, even as late as mid-1987 foreign trust banks had been able to capture less than one per cent of the corporate trust business and had barely touched the pension market;[35] prospects in the long term, however, look bright. By the mid-1980s, the Japanese Ministry of Finance had granted securities licences to foreign banks, a right denied to Japan's own banks which were still subject to Article 65 of the Exchange Law separating banking from securities. Foreigners have also been able to circumvent restrictions by having licences held by their subsidiaries or affiliates—witness broking units like that part owned by the Deutsche Bank and Security Pacific. To comply with the law, securities branches are only 50 per cent owned by the banks in question.[36] Needless to say, Japanese banks have resented this intrusion and it is only a matter of time before they are given the same rights. It may well be that in the long term Japanese institutions will profit from learning the practices of European trust banks and securities houses.

The slow pace of deregulation, due to Japanese reluctance to face competition in this field, has led to Western pressure to open the Tokyo Stock Exchange to foreigners. In December 1987, subsidiaries of the British banks, National Westminster, Kleinwort Grieveson, Schroder and Baring, were admitted to the Exchange—joining Warburg, the only completely British broker and a member there since 1985. Another route into the Tokyo Exchange is to buy a stake in a Japanese stockbroking firm, the first to do so being Foreign and Colonial, one of Britain's oldest investment companies (which in 1988 entered into a joint venture, approved by the Japanese Ministry of Finance, with the Tokyo-based stockbroker, National Capital Managements, a subsidiary of the Matsushita Organisation, owners of Panasonic Television). The British partner will have total control of National Capital's investment strategy.[37]

Japanese houses were at the time better represented on the London Stock Exchange and to British and other Europeans Tokyo membership was well worthwhile, justifying the high cost of admission—a little over one billion yen in 1985—and enabling them to save the 27 per cent commissions formerly paid to Japanese members in respect to share transactions. But the attractiveness of the Tokyo Exchange may, in the short term at least, prove illusory for while Tokyo is the largest equity market in the world, it is full of restrictive practices, with over half the trading undertaken through a small number of brokers and most of the market dominated by the cross holdings of major companies and investing institutions. Insider trading, too, is a way of life in the Tokyo Exchange which does not have the British regulatory mechanisms, although legislation to curb malpractices is being proposed. Another obstacle to EC success is the cultural barriers—Japanese stress on personal relationships rather than institutional ones as well as Japanese investment philosophy. Knowledge in the modern world of economic change knows no national boundaries; foreign securities firms not only provide their clients with the skills to invest in Japan but also give Japanese investors the expertise to penetrate financial markets abroad. In sectors like futures, where foreign expertise remains pre-eminent and Japanese markets are still in their infancy, Tokyo authorities are timing the pace of development to allow domestic companies a chance to compete. As a measure of the limited Western success in Japanese financial markets to date, foreign securities firms handle only a tiny proportion of turnover in Tokyo.[38]

With perseverance Western companies can overcome these problems and economic trends in Japan offer rich opportunities. Successful Japanese trading and investment abroad have remoulded the world economic order; they are also bringing changes in Japan's own financial markets, especially in the realm of savings instruments. A major trend, already noted, is the securitisation of lending; in addition, industrial enterprises are borrowing less from banks and raising more equity capital. Hitherto banks have thrived on the low, controlled interest rates on deposits from private investors, and have thus been able to lend cheaply to industry but they will now be increasingly exposed to competition from other investment outlets. Nevertheless, as late as mid-1987 about 70 per cent of all deposits in general in Japan were in regulated accounts like those in banks.[39] By 1986 the Ministry of Finance had deregulated interest rates on deposits over 300 million yen, and as this trend is extended to smaller deposits, investors will have more outlets for their savings. The banks, of course, will try to hold their own by using higher interest rates to attract and keep funds.

These trends must be seen in conjunction with other recent reforms, notably those concerning accounts held in the state-run postal savings banks which have long put the commercial banks at a disadvantage. The banks had always sniped at 'maruyu', the system of tax exemption on postal savings on which a slightly higher rate of interest was permitted. This was because these funds were channelled into the government's special infrastructure budget for use by national development agencies. The system had, however, been subject to abuse through investors having multiple accounts, and tax relief was to be abolished in relation to certain key categories of depositor as from April 1988. This measure could cut both ways; the Post Office will lose one advantage but may in other respects benefit by being forced to compete with the banks.

With these and other developments in Japan's financial markets, the outlook seems good for EC and other foreign banks and securities houses. In any case both banks and postal accounts are attracting a declining share of Japanese personal savings and there is a discernible move towards equities. In late 1987 Nomura (which accounts for much of the shares traded on the Tokyo Stock Exchange) estimated that the ratio of equities to investors' income will rise rapidly in the years to come; at present only one Japanese in fifteen invests directly in shares as opposed to one Briton in seven.[40] The number of individual Japanese shareholders has now reached 7.55 million or 6 per cent of the population; typically these are from the growing middle class like managers of small and medium-sized companies.[41] Furthermore there is a rapid accumulation of private pension and life insurance company funds, and restrictions on their investment in equities are being eased; currently less than a quarter of their assets are in shares compared with an equivalent British figure of 75 per cent.[42]

Not surprisingly, EC banks, brokers and fund managers are eager to enter Japanese financial markets. By the mid-1980s, for example, Lloyds Bank had opened an office in Tokyo to assist Japanese corporations to deal in the international capital markets and help those seeking fund-raising opportunities in Japan. Fund management in Japan is a specialist sector where the British can sell their skills to the Japanese, as investing Japanese funds in overseas equities is best done by foreign firms acquainted with Western markets.[43]

In summary, financial deregulation in Tokyo stemmed from both external and internal pressures. If Japanese capital exporters wanted to take full advantage of markets overseas, they could only do this through new legislation which at the same time offered some reciprocal concessions to foreign investors in Japan itself. Yet for EC countries to exploit fully the new opportunities in Japan, they must overcome cultural barriers like the reluctance of Japanese professionals to work for foreign firms which are now recruiting new Japanese graduates, some of whom have American MBA degrees, a notable example of this being the British company, Warburg. In this respect the British are in the vanguard as they have long been in the field of international investment. In the years to come a premium will be placed on knowledge of Japanese language and society on the part of foreigners and steps are already being taken in European universities to make good the deficiencies in this area. Cultural interaction is already leaving its mark on labour relations in Britain's Northeast where Japanese industrial ventures are well established; Japanese practices could eventually have an impact in the financial sphere too.

Influence is a two-way process, however, and the opening of Japanese consumer and capital markets to foreign competition is bringing about changes in Japan's own employment patterns. It has often been argued that Japan's post-war economic success derives from a social contract by which workers give of their loyalty in return for job security and lifetime tenure; the recruitment of management in the major corporations from generalists trained at Japan's elite universities is seen as another important factor. But financial deregulation requires new kinds of technical personnel because banks and securities houses are developing new lines of business which call for expertise, as in foreign exchange dealing, which is in short supply in Japan.[44] Economic restructuring is bringing into prominence the venture business— the small fast-growing company which develops its own technology and enjoys a large share of a specialist market. Innovation is now at a premium, and because their products contain much innovative knowhow, venture businesses usually spend far more on research and development in relation to sales than larger established companies. With slower growth in Japanese 'smoke-stack' industries like steel, automobiles and electrical goods, promotion opportunities are more limited, and there is therefore greater labour mobility, often into entrepreneurial sectors. Venture businesses are also benefiting from tax concessions and a buyer's market for loans; city banks are now inclined to offer loans more on the criterion of high technology than collateral alone. Together with major firms, these small ventures will play a crucial role in the creation of a new generation of industries for the twenty-first century.[45]

These new technological needs have prompted a reassessment of Japan's education system and its philosophy derived from China's Confucianism. This was a theory of knowledge which placed a greater emphasis on individual commitment and performance than on natural intelligence. In other words, with no effort spared, any person could become one of the elect, and this attitude, along with the social contract, helped to bring about Japan's post-war economic success. The other side of the coin, however, has been stress on rote learning in many subjects, though this stemmed from the need for the Japanese child initially to learn by heart complicated 'kanji', or Chinese characters, the basis of the Japanese written language. Now these learning habits are under fire; the Japanese education system has been meritocratic and competitive but, in the view of some, in the wrong way. This approach was all very well when Japan was importing foreign technology, imitating it and improving upon it but for oneself to innovate calls for a creative spirit. Thus Japanese schoolchildren can solve mathematical problems, through set formulae, but are weaker on logic; they are taught the techniques of passing examinations but do not become broadly educated or stimulated to new patterns of thought.[46]

The Japanese establishment is becoming increasingly aware that an innovative attitude is crucial; to give a simple example, software for computers will be of greater importance in the years to come than hardware, that is, electronics *per se*.[47] There are other aspects of Japan's philosophical and religious traditions that could help to promote innovation; Buddhism is a faith which, in stressing the transitory nature of life, favours pragmatism and adjustment to change. But success in inculcating new attitudes also demands leadership, and in this vein the Japanese government in August 1984 set up a National Council on Educational Reform to advise Prime Minister Nakasone, and its First Report was submitted in mid-1985. The Council laid down basic principles for reform which included a regard for creativity, thinking ability and power of expression, a wider choice of subjects and stress on information technologies. These priorities are a tacit acknowledgement that international rivalry has shifted from competition for control over territory, trade and capital towards a struggle to acquire information and the most effective technology.[48] The Japanese can no longer rely on ideas borrowed from abroad, course structures must be flexible and university students in all subjects must become computer literate. MITI has already predicted that Japan will face a chronic lack of engineers and computer programmers by the end of the decade.[49]

Educationalists do not seem to tire of reminding EC governments, especially the British, that they have much to learn from the Japanese academic experience. But wherever its strengths, Japan's education system must surely be revamped to produce the new technical and financial personnel needed by the country's fastest growing economic sectors—witness the acute shortage of translators, economic analysts and public relations officers in major corporations. Not surprisingly Japan's Ministry of Justice now has the power to ease the immigration of young professionals hired by securities firms and English-language teachers.[50]

Thus, as in the economic and financial sectors, there is scope in the educational and cultural fields for Japan-EC co-operation. In early 1988 Japanese universities were in the market to buy land and facilities from financially hard-pressed British universities, the aim being to send students from Japan to study in Europe. These campuses could also in future provide for some of the children of Japanese nationals resident in Britain. Similarly, in recognition of the role of language in understanding, Japanese Studies Centres, both publicly and privately financed, have been established in individual EC countries, and similarly the Community has sent a number of young businessmen to Japan on training programmes.

In conclusion, there is a sense in which the idea of Japanese uniqueness—which fostered a narrow nationalism and yet helped to promote post-war economic recovery—had come to be seen, even by the Japanese, as outmoded by the mid-1980s with the realisation that the Japanese could only guarantee their future prosperity in a world of interdependence through opening their consumer goods and capital markets to foreign competition. Moreover, as the EC countries gained a greater understanding of the Japanese, they too came to believe that Japan's economic and financial systems were no longer impenetrable. It would be foolish to say that EC-Japan co-operation in these fields will be without friction but trade, investment and cultural exchange could well have a considerable impact on the societies of the EC countries and Japan by the end of this century.

6
Conclusion: Changing Perspectives

China and Japan each responded differently to the threat presented by the Western impact on Asia in the mid-nineteenth century but both sought to harness the technology of the West to regain or preserve their national sovereignty. While, however, the Chinese Imperial rulers faced an authority crisis—the inability to create political institutions effective enough to defend their country and promote economic development—Japan's Meiji oligarchs were able to enforce their own legitimacy and achieve national unity, mobilising the population for modernisation goals. The Chinese, though, never lost their identity in spite of their country's economic backwardness because of vast material resources and confidence in an age-old culture. The Japanese, however, while technologically advanced, have borrowed much from China and the Western world and to this day remain much less sure of their place in the world. These crises of authority and identity have helped to shape the relations of the two powers with the West, including those with the EC.

For many decades the Chinese world-view was characterised by anti-Imperialism and after 1949 by the CCP's avowed support for world revolution, especially armed insurrection in the developing countries of Asia, Africa and Latin America. In the post-Mao era, however, Deng Xiaoping and his associates have moved away from the rigid categories of friends and enemies—expounded in orthodox Marxism-Leninism—towards a more omni-directional and issue-oriented foreign policy. While the cause of ultimate world Communist revolution has not been abandoned, policies designed to turn China into an advanced industrial country have been given priority, economic development being seen as the bulwark of national security. Thus Chinese foreign policy has become economically motivated, flexible and pragmatic, being concerned with the balance of power in Asia and the world as a whole. In both economic and political terms the Chinese have a number of options and seek to avoid domina-

129

tion by any one power or powers. This is perhaps best demonstrated by Chinese moves towards an equidistant stance *vis-à-vis* the superpowers, policy tilting in the direction of a limited accord with the Soviet Union while not refusing rapprochement with the USA. There is no doubt that the euphoria of the early 1970s over the Sino-American relationship has cooled; in 1988 the Chinese objected to a US Defense Department decision to put them back on the list of countries considered hostile, even though this may not affect most mutual trade. To take the heat out of the border conflict and thus help reduce military spending, the Soviet leaders gave China concessions on the Amur River frontier in August 1987. Soviet willingness to include, in the INF Treaty with the West, medium-range missiles sited in Central Asia was also viewed favourably by the Chinese. Though from a small base, Sino-Soviet trade grew to over US$2 billion in 1986 and a major agreement was signed in 1988. This trade has several advantages, as some of it is in kind, thereby avoiding a drain on hard currency reserves, and it obviates the administrative problems of international trade. China imports from the USSR goods such as rolled steel, pig iron and machinery, and exports agricultural products and low-quality consumer commodities which are not easy to sell in sophisticated Western markets. In return, the Soviet Union has supplies which would otherwise need to be transported from Moscow, 4,000 miles away.[1]

In the 1970s and 1980s Japan has been China's major trading partner and a source of loans for development but in view of events in the 1930s and 1940s, the Chinese are reluctant to rely too heavily on this connection. In January 1988 the official *Beijing Review* claimed that approval by the Japanese government of a military budget (which again exceeded the one per cent limit) implied a revival of Japanese militarism. Thus the EC countries are regarded as a counterweight to the Japanese; indeed the cultivation of the latter was said by some foreign observers to have been a factor in the fall of Hu Yaobang, Deng Xiaoping's protégé and former CCP General Secretary, in 1987. Japanese loans have also become more expensive to repay with the appreciation in the value of the yen. It is in this context that we should view Chinese praise of co-operation in the economic, technological and military spheres among EC countries, as they speak with one voice in international affairs and become a countervailing force against any superpower hegemony.[2]

The Chinese, then, have a choice of economic partners but

whatever options they take they must ensure that their country offers attractive trade and investment opportunities. Until the 1970s China was a Marxist-Leninist command economy dominated by central planning and administrative controls rather than the entrepreneurial spirit, the profit motive and market forces, a situation not conducive to foreign economic co-operation. Reducing the central government's role in the economy, however, is also a political issue, and reform in the 1980s has come up against vested interests from the highest levels of the CCP to the lowest levels of the administrative hierarchy. China's leaders have been divided between the conservatives, like Chen Yun who caution against too rapid and thoroughgoing economic change, and the reformers, led by Deng Xiaoping, although even here there are differing views over methods and timing. In the context of this power struggle the April 1988 Session of the National People's Congress, China's parliament, may well prove a watershed, even though the proceedings and appointments which ensued were no doubt decided upon in the inner councils of the all-powerful CCP in the preceding weeks. In fact, decisions of the Congress confirmed trends that were already in being. Deng's protégé and heir apparent, Zhao Ziyang, the CCP's General Secretary, became Vice-chairman of the Central Military Commission, second only to Deng, thus strengthening his influence with the army, a powerful arbiter in Chinese politics. Other appointments reflected the reformers' ascendancy, even if the day-to-day practical task of restructuring fell to the newly-confirmed Premier Li Peng who, while not opposed to reform, favoured gradual not rapid change.

A major feature of the 1980s ongoing reform programme has been the close linkage between political change and economic reforms, and this has had to be justified in terms of Marxist-Leninist ideology on which the legitimacy of the CCP leaders is ultimately based. Thus to allow for the development of limited forms of capitalism, the concept of 'the initial stage of socialism' has been introduced, whereby collective and private forms of enterprise may coexist with the dominant state sector. Capitalism is considered an expedient and not an ideal, and the achievement of a mature socialist society could take a long time: meanwhile the priority is not the class struggle but the revamping of an obsolete production system to satisfy the material needs of a growing population. There are many roads to socialism, and capitalism itself has changed since Lenin's day.[3]

These ideas have been given substance in current reform measures. Given the maintenance of a one-party state, indirect macro-economic control is deemed necessary, the central government providing the proper conditions for development and economic co-operation with foreign countries. Accordingly, to provide greater efficiency, it was announced at the 1988 National People's Congress that government departments were being streamlined, with the abolition of fourteen ministries and commissions. While the reorganised State Economic and Planning Commissions will have charge of the Chinese economy as a whole, public and private enterprises are to be more independent in terms of their management and use of resources. In addition, Party and government bodies and their personnel are being subjected to a more clearly defined separation of powers: in enterprises, for example, the role of Party secretaries and committees, formerly dominant, is now reduced to general supervision; real power is devolved to factory directors and technical experts. This system is intended to lead to personnel recruitment on the basis of merit and technical expertise and in place of the lifelong tenure system hitherto enjoyed by cadres employed on the basis of political loyalty alone. Staff retention and promotion will be based not on seniority alone but on raising productivity. Economic performance will be judged in terms of efficiency and profits; the private sector is recognised as complementary to the socialist sector of the economy with its own rights and interests. While ideological purists would attack these measures as unsocialist, the reformers accept the need to sacrifice egalitarian social goals for the demands of a developing economy, and their message is unmistakable: the reforms of the past ten years will not be reversed and foreign companies may be assured of the safety of their investments in a China where enterprise is now rewarded.[4]

These reforms of the 1980s have been designed to make the Chinese economy more efficient, thereby promoting export competitiveness and improving the conditions for more foreign investment. But while in the long run these reforms may work, they are producing some undesirable side-effects in the short run giving rise to popular dissatisfaction which China's conservatives may attempt to exploit. The most obvious of these has been inflation which is anathema to a nation accustomed to decades of price stability under a command economy. Indeed, one of the original popular appeals of the CCP leaders was their promise to halt the rampant inflation of the Civil War period of the late 1940s. The issue is a sensitive one; the Chinese reformers want to make the economy more responsive to market forces both at home and abroad but they dare not risk the disapproval of the populace who might be quick to blame foreigners and the 'open-door' policy for current ills. Consequently, in the late 1980s the CCP has been forced to maintain subsidies and rationing for certain foods in order to hold down prices which have tended to rise on account of a relative decline in agricultural productivity. Measures like the 'household responsibility system' following the rural reform programme of 1978–79 have proved a mixed blessing: the release of peasant initiative through private farming as opposed to collectives helped agricultural output as a whole to rise by about 8 per cent during 1981–85 but the acreage devoted to grain began to fall and productivity per acre was slow to rise.[5] By 1987 grain output was falling short of its target, and compensating imports were double the 1986 figure. One aim of the agricultural reforms had been crop diversification both for the domestic and export markets but once given the choice, Chinese farmers elected to grow cash crops like tropical fruit for the free markets because they were more profitable than growing grain. Moreover, dismantling the collectives led to the division of land into strips which reduces the scope for mechanisation and large-scale irrigation needed to boost output. The peasants' natural conservatism has also reasserted itself.

The thrust of rural policy since 1983 suggests that the CCP leaders see the remedy for lagging grain production to lie in the consolidation of holdings into larger units. Technically, all land is owned by the state but a 1984 regulation allowed land to be contracted out for periods of up to fifteen years. In April 1988 the National People's Congress took this process a stage further; a constitutional amendment permitted cultivators to sell land rights (even though the state still owns the land) thereby facilitating the accumulation of landholdings to achieve economies of scale. A more efficient agriculture will also require less manpower; by the end of 1984 it was estimated that a quarter of the rural labour force was in non-agricultural pursuits like commerce and local small-scale industrial enterprises.[6]

In sum, higher agricultural productivity through economies of scale and the better use of technology and manpower could obviate the need for subsidies, these being considered expedient by the current leadership who wish to let market forces control supply and demand—but not at the cost of inflated food prices in the cities, (rises thought by some foreign observers to be running as high as 20 per cent) and urban unrest.

In this period of transition from the use of administrative

control to reliance on market forces the pricing of industrial raw materials and products has been as unrealistic (if not more so) than that of foods and agricultural produce. It has been officially admitted that excessive rises in commodity prices are a major problem and that the pricing structure can only be re-formed gradually, with subsidies continuing indefinitely. In fact, it has been much easier to introduce incentives in agriculture than in industry; individual peasant households develop an emo-tional tie to their land and can more readily see the fruits of their labour. In contrast, there is less accountability in industry which has a bureaucracy spreading from the central government ministries to factory directors and managers. Furthermore, in spite of the devolution of powers, controls still operate in areas such as raw material supplies. Even more difficult to reform than economic institutions *per se* are bureaucratic attitudes born of entrenched vested interests.

Industrial reforms are having some success, however, and as in the case of agriculture, current difficulties have been taken by the reformers as a cue not for reversal but for further change. One example is the 'economic zone' policy (to be distinguished from the Special Economic Zone discussed earlier on) to get more co-operation between local regions and between enter-prises. A case in point is the Shanghai Economic Zone, established in 1982 and later expanded to cover the provinces of Jiangsu, Zhejiang, Anhui, Jiangxi and Fujian, including the Special Zone of Xiamen. While the creation of these zones is still in the experi-mental stage, the general objectives are clear. Prior to China's 'open-door' policy industrial and commercial activity was verti-cally organised, with enterprises operating under the jurisdiction of ministries such as Machine Building, according to their sector of production. These administrative hierarchies tended to be watertight, and there was little, if any, co-operation between re-gions or enterprises. Recent reforms have encouraged the cre-ation of economic associations which cut across administrative and provincial boundaries. These arrangements are intended to permit the national exploitation of local natural resources through enterprise initiative as well as the formation of regional economic structure based on industrial specialisation and division of labour. After the establishment of the Shanghai Economic Zone the Ministries of Machine Building transferred their jurisdiction over enterprises to large cities and local regions; government administration was thus separated from business operations. In this way the economic zone policy strengthens horizontal ties among enterprises as well as facilitating the creation of economic associations amongst different industries (though provincial and municipal government offices and bureaux still retain some administrative controls over enterprises under their jurisdiction). The economic zones and associations are intended to foster competitiveness among enterprises and the nation-wide distribution of goods; prior to the reforms of the 1980s enterprises had a virtual monopoly in the provinces in which they were located.[7]

Of note, too, is that while private entrepreneurship in industry is still in its infancy in China, the leasing of ailing factories to individuals is being pioneered in the northern city of Shenyang and has met with a fair degree of success.[8]

Such restructuring has been directed towards producing a more secure and stable environment for foreign trade and investment, especially in view of the overheating of the economy in 1985. Imbalances in the economy were partly due to the rapid pace of the reforms themselves. Industrial investment, for example, ran well over state targets that year and imports grew far more rapidly than exports, giving rise to a serious trade deficit which was repeated in 1986 when it stood at nearly US$12 billion. The government then adopted measures like reducing import levels and tightening foreign exchange controls. In July 1986 the Chinese currency, the yuan, was devalued by 15.8 per cent against major currencies. By 1987, the economic squeeze was having some effect; exports rose by 29 per cent but imports by only 2.2 per cent, resulting in a lower overall trade deficit of just under US$4 billion. The CCP leaders were also aware of the threats of protectionism in the EC and the USA, which could slow down China's economic growth. In addition, both China's manufactured goods (which were playing an increasing role in China's exports) and her agricultural products like cereals, edible oils and specialist commodities like medicines would have to compete with similar products from other developing countries. Clearly, the trade battle had been fought on two fronts; all but essential imports must be curbed and efforts made to ensure Chinese goods were competitive on world markets.

China's economic priorities and her trade structure should nevertheless give EC traders grounds for cautious optimism. During the early and middle 1980s many of China's imports were capital goods needed to upgrade transportation, energy supplies and communications, sectors which were holding back economic development, and EC countries were the major suppliers. In fact, in 1986 the EC as a whole was China's third largest trading partner (after Japan and Hong Kong), total trade being worth US$11.6 billion. The Community was then supplying 45 per cent of China's advanced technology imports and had become China's second largest supplier of advanced technology and equipment. The Japanese, in contrast, export more industrial plants and equipment to China than the EC and are accused by the Chinese of being reluctant to transfer technology.[9]

Among EC countries the Federal Republic of Germany was pre-eminent, accounting for between US$3 and 4 billion of trade with China in 1986. The Chinese, however, maintain their practice of diversifying sources of supply; in the field of energy, for instance, the British firm, John Brown Engineering, won turnkey contracts worth £45 million with China's Ministry of Petroleum in connection with power generation at three of China's oil installations.[10] It has been the dream of Western traders since the nineteenth century to penetrate the vast Chinese market, and this can become a reality if EC exporters target relevant sectors; the strengths of British industry, for example, lie in energy, telecommunications, transport, agriculture and industrial modernisation, all of which are priorities in China's development strategy. Trade in the middle and late 1980s has been heavily in favour of the EC countries. The important factor is China's capacity to pay but with the growing willingness of the Chinese leaders to borrow abroad—witness the US$5.5 billion China borrowed from the World Bank during 1981–87 for investment in fifty-two projects and a further loan of US$12 billion from the same source announced in March 1988 for the years up to 1992—prospects seem bright for continuing EC-China trade and economic co-operation.[11]

Since the initiation of the 'open-door' policy in the late 1970s China has become a pioneer among communist countries in accepting investment from the West and this had been given a key role in China's economic development strategy. China's leaders have set themselves the task of raising all sectors of the economy by the end of the century to the levels reached by developed countries during the 1970s and 1980s. Not only is there a need for technology transfers but also for the wherewithal to transform about 400,000 antiquated Chinese enterprises. Giving scope for foreign investment, the National People's Congress of April 1988 designated virtually all of China's seaboard from Hainan Island in the south to the southern tip of Manchuria in the north as ripe for integration into the international economy, charging it with the task of processing imported raw materials and selling finished products back on the world market. The aim is to emulate the post-war economic miracles of Singapore and Taiwan.[12]

Between 1980 and 1986 China absorbed about US$6 billion in foreign investment; over 7,000 enterprises took part in this, 80 per cent of which were in the coastal region. Nevertheless, EC investment in China has been slow and cautious, and is much less in value than from Hong Kong, the USA and Japan. Percentages of total investment for the period from 1979 to 1985 were as follows—Hong Kong, 80 per cent; the United States, 8 per cent; Japan 7 per cent; Europe (including mainly the EC), 4 per cent. A few examples will suffice to indicate the range of EC investment projects, although the most significant of these may prove in the long term to lie in the energy and infrastructure sectors. One of the best known joint ventures was the automobile enterprise, Shanghai Volkswagen, jointly run by China and the Federal Republic of Germany. An example of venture co-operation is when the British steel company GKN announced, through its West German subsidiary Uni-Cardon, the formation of the Shanghai GKN Drive Shaft Company, designed to supply components for the Volkswagen Santana model, already being built under licence in China.[13]

Several EC countries have been active in oil exploration, although findings so far have been disappointing. By late 1986 Total of France's Weizhou field in the Gulf of Beibu had come on stream but the output hardly justified operating costs. That energy resource exploration has a payoff only in the long term was acknowledged by an international consortium (including British Petroleum and Nippon Oil) which expressed an interest in China's north-east Xinjiang region; reserves there could be huge but production was unlikely before the turn of this century in view of high transportation costs to a remote desert location.[14]

It has become a cliché to say that the modern mass media have turned the world into a global village but there is no doubt that exposure to Western systems will have a far-reaching impact on closed societies like in China. The British firm, Cable and Wireless, has agreed on a joint venture with Hong Kong's Whampoa and the China International Trust and Investment Corporation—a banking arm of the Chinese government—to launch the first domestic telecommunications satellite to cover China for use in connection with television programmes.[15]

These are but a few instances but they give some idea of the range of EC investment, the conditions for which still often appear unfavourable, especially in view of lingering central government controls over labour mobility and the movement of foreign currency as well as low productivity and high production costs. Experiments in zones like Shenzhen, conceived of as pacesetters for the rest of the Chinese economy, are nevertheless pioneering reforms based on market demand, freer hiring of workers and a tendering system for contracts. Being insulated from the rest of China, the zones soften the impact of foreign capital, technology and currency on the structure of China's economy. They are significant in a social sense too; they slow down the influence of Western values on Chinese society as a whole, so that rising expectations among the Chinese populace can be more easily contained.[16] Coastal cities like Shanghai also have the advantages of a better trained work-force, a good material supply base and communications with the interior. Providing EC companies are as export-oriented as the Chinese leaders would wish, they can profit from cheap labour and abundant indigenous raw materials.

Barriers to the continued expansion of foreign investment are partly institutional and partly cultural. Factors such as the price reforms in the urban industrial sector have not yet gone far enough and there are too the 'intangibles' such as the values of Western-style legal systems. EC and other foreign investors want guarantees that their assets in China will not be nationalised at some future date and want agreements to be clearly defined. The Foreign Economic Contract Law of the People's Republic of China, promulgated in 1985, was a step in the right direction, even though it included one-sided provisions such as those requiring wholly foreign-owned enterprises to make use of advanced technology and to market most of their products outside China. Chinese laws remain inadequate for the conduct of international business, at least in the eyes of potential foreign partners.

If lack of an adequate legal process impedes foreign cooperation, Chinese management practices hamper China's industrial progress. Conscious of this weakness, the Chinese leaders created the Chinese Management Association (CEMA) in 1979 to tackle this problem at a national level, and in 1983 an agreement was made with the EC to initiate a new two-year Master of Business Administration (MBA) course under its auspices. The assumption was that poor management attitudes stifled economic reform. Under the command economy, where there was central planning and a seller's market, the emphasis was on achieving output targets; enterprise managers were not required to develop marketing skills, make business policy like their Western counterparts and see to quality control. Both the Confucian tradition and Marxism-Leninism have a built-in anti-capitalist ethos; true value is created by the production of goods, and profit-making merchants, middlemen and distributors are social parasites. These beliefs are not conducive to the development of marketing skills, Western-type financial practices and distribution services. The Chinese have had a different conception of what constitutes a good manager, and with increasing enterprise autonomy and international competition they find themselves short of personnel versed in sound management knowhow. It is in this area that EC business-school experts are playing a crucial role.

It is not merely a matter, however, of transplanting EC or other Western management techniques in China since there also has to be more cultural interaction between China and the West. In China even professional relationships are still very personalised whereas in the West competence and efficiency are prized as much as connections *per se*. In time, increasing stress on the accountability of individual managers will make for more professionalism and less reliance on connections for their own sake. EC business schools impart management skills through the seminar method of discussion between staff and students on an equal footing, a system rather at odds with the Confucian and Chinese Communist education systems where truth is handed down from on high by the teacher. The Chinese have several options among EC management programmes and may well be influenced by more than one of these. Ultimately, however, institutional reforms based on capitalist ideas will affect Chinese cultural values and attitudes, though not destroy them: in time the Chinese may evolve management practices that are inspired by both traditional Chinese-type relationships and Western techniques and adapted to China's own conditions and requirements.[17]

In these respects China may become like Japan, a country which has preserved many of its traditional social patterns while learning from the West. But though during the last century and a half the Japanese have created effective structures at home to deal with the Western challenge, they are only just beginning to define their role in an increasingly multi-polar world, where the economies of the two superpowers, the USA and the USSR, are in relative decline. Thus although by the late 1980s Japan had the world's second highest national income after the USA, its political confidence has not matched its economic power. This has prompted the familiar argument (among critics in the US Congress, for example) that the Japanese have enjoyed a free ride on defence, refusing to shoulder their share of the Western Alliance's military burden. Partly in response to this complaint the Nakasone Cabinet in 1987 lifted the one per cent limit on defence spending. By NATO criteria (which include items like military pensions) Japanese expenditure had actually exceeded this limit some years earlier. The Japanese have now agreed to guarantee the security of the Pacific sea lanes up to a thousand miles from Japan, although it is still understood that an attack on Japan would activate an American response under the Mutual Security Treaty.   Some in Japan are concerned lest there be circumstances in which Americans might not see it in their interest to defend Japan in a war with the Soviet Union, and this view is shared by some EC politicians in the context of their countries' own defence arrangements with the USA. These concerns have not been lessened by increased Soviet military presence in Asia, particularly in the Gorbachev era; in Vladivostok in July 1986 the Soviet leader stressed that he placed no less importance on Asia than on Europe. Between 1976 and 1987 Soviet ground forces in the Far East were increased from 31 to 43 divisions, naval strength grew from 755 to 840 vessels and the number of combat aircraft went up by more than 300. Nuclear-capable forces deployed by the Soviet Union in the Far East stood at 170 SS20 missiles and 85 TU22 backfire bombers by 1987: none of these weapons were present in 1976. From 1986 the Soviet military presence in Asia has been reinforced with up-to-date SU27 and Mig31 long-range jet fighters.[18] And there is still the contentious issue of the Northern Islands, claimed by Japan but occupied by the Soviet Union since 1945 and latterly reinforced by installations monitoring Japanese and American military movements.

Accordingly, by 1987 Japan's defence strategy was being reappraised, albeit within the context of the US nuclear umbrella. The atomic attacks on Hiroshima and Nagasaki in 1945 led to strong pacifist sentiments in Japan but public opinion has been slowly changing and is now more inclined to support the Liberal Democratic Party (LDP) and the Defence Agency who call for more Japanese independence in defence matters. To achieve this, emphasis is being placed on deploying the airforce and navy to intercept invaders before they reach Japan rather than relying on the army to engage the enemy on Japanese soil, a strategy which will require substantial increases in expenditure. Guide-lines set down in January 1987 allow unlimited defence budgets from 1991 onwards, domestic parliamentary opposition notwithstanding, and in 1988–89 military spending was raised by 5.2 per cent to £10 billion, placing Japan high in the world league. An implicit assumption behind Japanese defence thinking is that an invasion of Japan could occur at a time when the USA was otherwise engaged in handling a military crisis in the Middle East or Western Europe.[19]

The Japanese hope that their more independent defence posture will meet with approval in Europe. EC and Japanese security interests do not always coincide, however, as each side competes for US protection. Thus although the final INF Treaty eliminating medium-range missiles pleased the Japanese, they remember that initially the USA had agreed to removing these weapons from Europe while permitting the Soviet Union to maintain them in Asia. The Japanese reckon that shouldering a greater share of their own defence burden will give them a greater voice in Western defence councils.[20]

It is within this setting that Japanese diplomatic initiatives in the late 1980s must be viewed, especially with regard to the EC. In seeking to reduce their dependence on the USA and accepting more responsibility for their own defence, the Japanese have realised that they must also seek other markets, since protectionist calls from the US Congress are still made from time to time. One result has been huge world-wide Japanese trade surpluses which are viewed with apprehension by the EC.

The Japanese Prime Minister's statements during a visit to EC capitals in May 1988 may nevertheless indicate Japanese awareness of the Community's potential influence in trade. In 1992 the EC will become a unified single market when internal barriers are removed, and this might be accompanied by the creation of external barriers against Japanese goods. The full implication of '1992' is political union, although this is no doubt a long way off; meanwhile the Japanese see the EC as an emerging economic superpower and part of an anti-communist group which includes the USA and Japan. Mr Takeshita's visit was thus designed to reinforce cultural and political ties with the EC in the light of Japan's enormous economic stake in the Community. Britain, for instance, has benefited from the presence of about seventy Japanese manufacturing firms in Britain employing over 20,000 workers, and Japan is already the second largest investor in Britain after the USA. There have been other less tangible, though nonetheless real, benefits; industrial harmony in joint ventures has been attributed to the Japanese labour-relations system, and new Japanese technology has been brought in to the country.[21]

EC countries have already gained much from the Japanese connection; they could still exert more pressure in their attempts to persuade Japan's leaders to be more amenable over issues such as trade surpluses and remaining Japanese tariffs. Concessions are in Japan's long-term interest, and the lines of communication must be kept open. One European concern is to see that the expansion of Japanese domestic demand continues, as promised by Mr Takeshita, in order to reduce the Japanese trade surplus with the EC. From the EC angle, the 1987 figures were encouraging; while Japanese exports to the EC rose by nearly 20 per cent to nearly US$40 billion, Japanese imports from the EC climbed by 31 per cent to nearly US$20 billion, major increases being recorded by European sales of cars and textiles.[22] Increased Japanese imports of manufactured goods, of course, result from the higher living standards and greater spending power of the Japanese.

In fact, Japan's growing prosperity offers considerable opportunity for European exporters. The figures quoted above are for the Community as a whole and some EC countries have greater deficits with Japan than others. Take the case of Britain. Her exports to Japan rose by 25 per cent in 1987 over the previous year and were worth £1.5 billion. At the same time Japanese exports to Britain grew by 11 per cent to £5.4 billion, leaving a sizeable (visible) deficit of £4 billion, which was partly offset by a UK surplus in invisibles of about £2 billion. Other EC countries like the Federal Republic of Germany have been more successful in their trade with Japan.[23] In 1988 there remained bilateral issues like Britain's demand that the Japanese reduce the tax on Scotch whisky imports—a levy which is discriminatory in the eyes of GATT—and the continued reluctance to admit more British firms to membership of the Tokyo Stock Exchange. It is clear, however, that if opportunities are to be exploited further, there must be concerted EC action at Community level to prise open the Japanese market.

In fact, there are now fewer discriminatory tariffs on European goods and there are signs that the two parties are moving towards broader long-term co-operation. In early 1988 a Japanese agreement to give American companies preferential access to Japan's public works projects aroused EC fears that this would be at the expense of the Community, apprehension only being partially dispelled when a terminal contract for the new Kansai International Airport near Osaka was won by a French firm.[24] To take another instance. EC shipbuilders have long suffered from the lower prices charged by the Japanese and South Koreans, and in April 1988 EC officials and Japan's Transport Ministry took steps towards market sharing by establishing a committee to help monitor ship prices and alleviate the effects of economic depression in the world's shipyards.[25]

In the wake of Japan's new defence strategy arms manufacture by Japan or equipment sales to Japan could play a part in reducing US and EC trade deficits, even if a more heavily armed Japan is viewed by some with suspicion, especially in China and South-east Asia. Japan has huge potential for a defence industry; it already manufactures many of its own weapons, although some of them, like fighter aircraft, are still made under licence from US firms. Electronics can have both civilian and military uses, and the US in Vietnam used precision bombs guided by a Sony-made television camera. In addition, whereas in most countries civilian and military sectors are clearly separated, in Japan this division is not stringent and the exchange of personnel and technology is quite common.[26] Manufacture of weapons whether for Japanese use or export could be a hedge against recession; as the Japanese move out of certain industries—in deference to, say, EC complaints about trade surpluses—alternative employment could then be found for displaced Japanese workers. In turn, arms, but fewer other Japanese products, would be exported.

In certain military sectors, EC countries have greater strengths and more experience than the Japanese. In line with changes in their maritime defence policy the Japanese were, in early 1988, considering the purchase of a British-designed aircraft carrier like the *Invincible,* equipped with Sea Harrier planes and helicopters. This would be built in Japan but be based on British design and technology, bringing new business to Britain's warship builders who were faced with fewer orders from the British Ministry of Defence.[27]

Japan's post-war constitution prohibits the despatch of Japanese forces abroad but it has not prevented them from taking part in training exercises in the Pacific nor has it ruled out rearmament for defence purposes. The recent build-up must be seen in terms of the Japanese taking greater responsibility for their own defence in line with their country's growing political commitment and enhanced economic power.

Taking a broader and longer-term view, however, there are several kinds of economic co-operation such as in investment, joint ventures and exchange of technology, by which EC-Japan trade friction may be lessened. The Japanese have sought to get round EC barriers by targeting countries like Britain as sites for investment in manufacturing, especially electronics. In April 1988 Sharp announced a new components plant in North Wales, offering employment in an economically depressed area. The Japanese presence in Wales, though, has not passed without allegations (at Community level) of 'dumping'; firms have been accused of operating 'screwdriver' plants which assemble products from parts that are made cheaply outside Europe (mainly in Asia) and then market them in the EC. In early 1988 the Commission imposed fines on four Japanese typewriter companies: Silver Reed, Sharp, Canon and Kyushu Matsushita for 'screwdriver' practices which had given them unfair advantages over other EC manufacturers. Some Japanese undertakings like Brother Industries avoid duty or penalties by ensuring that the Japanese content of goods is below the 60 per cent set by the EC as the upper limit for non-EC components.

EC exporters have complained not only of Japanese tariff walls but of non-tariff barriers like distribution systems based on long-standing personal ties, more pronounced in Japan than elsewhere and seemingly impenetrable. One answer is for EC companies to set up their own distribution systems or engage in joint marketing with their Japanese counterparts. In March 1988 Guinness decided to set up its own distribution network in Japan, profits being enhanced by cutting out middlemen. Two operations are involved: the first, a joint venture including the French firm, Möet-Hennessy, will create the largest imported spirits operation which will employ 230 people; the second entails collaboration in Japan with a Japanese company to market both Scotch and Japanese whisky.[28] Should Japanese liquor tariff barriers be lowered, these operations will become even more profitable.

The above are just some examples of on-going EC-Japan economic co-operation. Such relationships are in future likely to be based on horizontal trade, that is to say, each side will move into those manufacturing sectors to which it is best suited by virtue of its resources and skills. From the Japanese side this is already being pursued by economic restructuring and the expansion of domestic demand. Like Japan, each country in the EC has its own particular strengths in science and technology, and these may be shared to mutual advantage. Japanese investment in Britain has created the impression that technological transfer is a one-way process; but British superiority in certain fields is reflected in the recent agreement between the government-owned British Technology Group (BTG) and Sumitomo Corporation, a leading Japanese company. Under the terms of the agreement Sumitomo becomes sole agent in Japan for licensing selected inventions in fields like engineering, electronics, computer software and new materials, thus facilitating their transfer to Japanese companies.[29]

Japanese goods have become household names in Europe and EC products will receive more and more recognition in Japan. Deregulation of Japanese financial markets has only just begun but Japan's institutions are already prominent in Western markets like London; and these banking and securities activities are a kind of reconnaissance operation designed to acquire new skills and experience. Hitherto, institutions like the Tokyo Stock Exchange have been tightly controlled, and the development of new skills was not needed by the Japanese in their own market. The pattern is changing as Japanese financial institutions are deregulated and become more international. Moreover, more and more EC investors are buying stocks and shares on the Tokyo Stock Exchange which—because of close regulation, limits on share price movements and corporate cross-holdings—was less badly hit by October 1987's 'Black Monday' than other exchanges. An easy credit policy by the Japanese government and a buoyant market made the Tokyo Exchange an attractive prospect for EC investors in 1988.[30]

Economic and financial interdependence among nations means that superpower status is increasingly difficult to define. Territorial possessions, access to material resources and a nuclear arsenal are still determinants of position in the world, but political power is coming to depend more on the acquisition of information through communications technologies, knowledge and education which know no national boundaries. In future, there are likely to be not two but several superpowers. In addition to the USA and the USSR, these will include China, Japan and the EC, the latter moving slowly towards political as well as economic unity. As the twentieth century draws to a close, the EC countries cannot but become involved economically, diplomatically and culturally with China and Japan, the two major powers in the Asia-Pacific region which is also the fastest growing economic area in the world.

Postscript

In a world becoming increasingly accustomed to the economic and political reforms associated with glasnost in Communist countries, student demonstrations in China during June 1989 were a sharp reminder that such reforms can only be successful over the long term and their implementation is itself fraught with difficulties.

Economic reforms as well as increased foreign trade and travel abroad have created among China's populace, especially the intelligentsia, rising expectations of which the events of June 1989 may be considered a by-product. In addition, current disagreement within the leadership over how severely to punish dissent parallels divisions over the nature and extent of economic reform. In the wake of such indecision, stemming partly from the apparent ill health of China's leader, Deng Xiaoping, hardline conservatives who wish to reduce the pace of economic change appear to be in the ascendant, and reformers like Zhao Ziyang (Deng's hand-picked successor and Chinese Communist Party General Secretary until mid-1989) have been accused of aiding and abetting the forces of counter-revolution.

Such divisions within the leadership over the nature and extent of reform were reflected in the replacement of Zhao as CCP General Secretary by Jiang Zemin. In late 1989, the policy of economic retrenchment was intensified in response to mounting inflation as well as serious budget and external deficits.

At the same time attempts are being made to discredit the reformers by linking them with those in the Party and state organs accused of corruption and nepotism as well as illegally profiting from foreign trade contacts.

Given the advanced age of Deng and his associates (including the conservatives), an incipient succession struggle seemed to be looming by August 1989. Deng, however, was still nominally in control of the campaigns against corruption and so-called counter-revolutionaries, although a decision on how to deal with the dismissed Zhao was still pending—the danger being that discrediting the latter might not only affect the Party's image abroad but damage Deng's own reputation as the self-appointed initiator of economic reform and the open-door policy.

At the time of writing, there remained other powerful factors suggesting that economic reform and limited political liberalisation were unlikely to be reversed. Introduced in August 1989 and designed to inculcate loyalty to Party and State rather than permit Western-style freedoms, measures such as increased political education, military training and manual labour for prospective university students and graduates—reminiscent of the Cultural Revolution—will no doubt continue as will policies of austerity to curb inflation. But ultimately such action on both the ideological and economic fronts must be considered as a temporary solution to the problems of success, and in spite of appearances to the contrary, the real debate in China must surely be not whether to reform or not but how far and how fast; divisions over policy may in any case conceal power and personality conflicts.

In the short term there may be attempts to contain the spread of Western ideas and influence so that demands for Western-style freedoms do not get out of control. For example, special Economic Zones like Shenzhen and Xiamen have been designated as channels for the introduction of foreign technology and know-how, and yet these are to a great extent insulated from the rest of China so that the spread of Western culture from these zones is limited. That the work-force and general population in these zones are quite content with rising living standards and the expectation of further gains could augur well for the future.

While the events of June 1989 have had an adverse effect on tourism, there is as yet little, if any, evidence to indicate that foreign trade and investment in China will be badly affected over the long term. Perhaps too many in China and the West have a stake in the open-door policy for it to be abandoned.

Finally, as representatives of a major power in the international community, China's leaders cannot be indifferent to foreign reaction to the policies they pursue both at home and abroad: they are more than ever before subject to the judgements of Western observers.

Notes

Chapter 1

1. See, for example, an article by Qi Wenhuan, 'The Trend of Western Europe to Become Independent of the United States' in *Beijing Shijie Zhishi* (World Knowledge), No. 8, 16 April 1983, pp. 10–12, as translated in *Joint Publications Research Service* (hereafter *JPRS*) 10 February 1984.

2. 'Spadolini and PRC's Zhang Aiping Sign Defence Agreement', *JPRS*, 29 April 1985.

3. For a discussion of these objectives, see the relevant article by Chiima Kiyofiku in the *Japan Quarterly*, January–March 1986, p. 13.

4. These figures were given in *Guoji Wenti Yanjiu*, No. 3., 13 July 1984, as reproduced in *JPRS*, 11 September 1984.

5. These matters are discussed in an article by Yuan Yuzhong, 'The Fluctuating Stability of the Situation in the Asian Pacific Area', *Beijing Shiji Zhishi*, No.9, 1 May 1984, pp. 2–5.

Chapter 2

1. Obstacles to the Chinese leaders' reform policies are described in Zhu Fu'en and others, 'One of the Obstacles to Reform: Analysis of the Force of Habit' in *Shehui Kexue*, No. 9., 15 September 1984, pp. 7–8, as translated in *JPRS*, 8 January 1985.

2. Masaharu Hishida, 'The Logic of Economic Reform', JETRO *China Newsletter*, No.57, July-August 1985, pp. 5–6; see also Kiichi Mochizuki, 'Chinese, Soviet and Hungarian Economic Reforms Compared', JETRO *Chinese Newsletter*, No.54, January-February 1985, pp. 7–10.

3. This issue is referred to in Jan Prybyla, 'China's Economic Experiment: from Mao to Market', *Problems of Communism*, January-February 1986, pp. 21–38.

4. These developments are noted in David Dodwell, 'A Dramatic Rise in Production: Agriculture', *Financial Times*, 9 December 1985.

5. An excellent in-depth analysis of industrial enterprise reform appears in Akira Fujimoto, 'China's Economic Reforms: The New Stage', JETRO *China Newsletter*, No.54, January-February 1985, pp. 2–6.

6. This information is drawn from Katsuhiko Hama, 'Distribution Reform in Guangdong Province', ibid., No.55, March-April 1985, p. 9.

7. Akira Fujimoto, 'China's Economic Reforms: The New Stage', ibid., No.54, January-February 1985, pp. 2–6.

8. Chinese economic performance in the mid-1980s is discussed in Satoshi Imai, 'Chinese Economy Sustains High Growth', ibid., No.55, March-April 1985, pp. 2–4.

9. Report by Mary Lee in *The Times*, 13 August 1985.

10. Issues of 'overheating' and inflation are discussed by Satoshi Imai, 'Cooling China's Overheating Economy', JETRO *China Newsletter,* No.61, March-April 1986, pp. 2–7.

11. For an excellent analysis of the Chinese price system and attempts at reform, see Kazuo Yamanouchi, 'The Chinese Price System and the Thrust of Reform', ibid., No.60, January-February 1986, pp. 2–11.

12. These reforms are discussed in Satoshi Imai, 'Cooling China's Overheated Economy', ibid., No.61, March-April 1986, pp. 2–7.

13. Jan Prybyla, 'From Mao to Market', *Problems of Communism,* Vol.XXXV, January-February 1986, pp. 21–38.

14. Some details presented here have been drawn from Seiichi Nakajima, 'China's Energy Policy Under the Seventh Five Year Plan', JETRO *China Newsletter,* No.59, November-December 1985, pp. 17–21.

15. Seiichi Nakajima, 'Reform of China's Transport System', ibid., No.55, March-April 1985, pp. 10–16.

16. See an article by a Chinese economist, Li Lin, 'Problems in the Introduction of Foreign Capital', ibid., No.62, May-June 1986, pp. 2–3.

17. Issues involved in these reforms are discussed in 'Call for Centralisation in Foreign Trade', *Beijing Jingji Ribao,* 3 March 1984, p. 2; a more critical analysis appears in Satoshi Imai, 'Reform of China's Foreign Trade System', JETRO *China Newsletter,* No.56, May-June 1985, pp. 2–7.

18. For details of the Hainan scandal, see *The Times,* 3 August 1985 and 3 September 1985.

19. These strategies are discussed in Hu Jun and Zhang Bingshen, 'Tentative Exploration of the Problem of Economic Development Zones', in *Guoji Maoyi Wenti* (International Trade Journal) No.6, November-December 1984, pp. 16–21, as translated in *JPRS,* 23 May 1985.

20. See Geoffrey Parkins, 'China Wants More Managers', *The Times Higher Education Supplement,* 2 August 1985. Rural management training is discussed by John N. Hawkins, 'The People's Republic of China', in R. Murray Thomas and T. Neville Postlethwaite, *Schooling in East Asia,* Pergamon Press, London, 1983.

21. For a detailed analysis of the educational reforms, see Geoffrey Parkins, 'China's Universities Help to Achieve Modernisation', in *The Times Higher Education Supplement,* 14 June 1986; also see his article, 'China Reconstructs for the 21st Century', in *ibid.,* 30 December 1985. Teacher Training Priorities are discussed in 'Changes in This Year's University Enrolment', *Renmin Ribao,* 11 May 1985. Details concerning the nine-year compulsory system appear in 'The Party Centre and the State Council Hold A National Educational Work Conference', *Renmin Ribao,* 16 May 1985.

Chapter 3

1. The key role of foreign trade is discussed in Fujiko Kitani, 'The Struggle to Expand Exports' in JETRO *China Newsletter,* No.63, July-August 1986, pp. 17–19.

2. For details, see Jean Quenon, 'Quality Management in China', *Euro-Asia Business Review,* Vol.5, No.3, July 1986, pp. 16–18.

3. A Western source pursuing this theme is Takashi Uehara, 'Computers in China', JETRO *China Newsletter,* No.55, March-April 1985, pp. 19–20.

4. A full commentary on 'administrative guidance' and 'reverse engineering' appears in an article by Sheng Jiqiu, 'How Postwar Japan Carried Out Technology Import', in Shijie Jingji (World Economy), No.10, 10 October 1984, pp. 68–73, as translated in *JPRS*, 30 April 1985.

5. Hiroko Kawai, 'China-Soviet Trade–The Present Situation and Outlook', JETRO *China Newsletter*, No.60, January-February 1986, pp. 16–17.

6. China-EC trade statistics have been drawn from the following sources: *China Daily*, 13 May 1985 and 16 May 1985; *Renmin Ribao*, 7 May 1985; Zhu Ruiqi, 'Bright Prospects for Enlarging China's Exports to the EC', *Guoji Maoyi* (Intertrade), No.6, 27 June 1984, pp. 18–19, as translated in *JPRS*, 16 June 1985, pp. 67–70.

7. Plant export figures are given in a special report published in JETRO *China Newsletter*, No.57, July-August 1985, p. 21.

8. For Sino-German trade trends, see *China Daily*, 10 June 1985; Jia Shi, 'Sino-FRG Economic and Trade Relations Have Made Rapid Progress in the Past Twelve Years', *Guoji Maoyi* (Intertrade), No.10, 27 October 1984, pp. 11–12, as translated in *JPRS*, 19 March 1985, pp. 58–61; 'Experience, State, and Perspectives in German-China Trade' in Wochen Bericht Des Deutschen Instituts Fuer Wirtshaftsforchung, 13 September 1984, pp. 470–6 in *JPRS*, 24 October 1984. The introduction of manufacturing technology into China is discussed in a special report on Sino-Japanese trade which appears in JETRO *China Newsletter*, No.62, May-June 1986, p. 17.

9. The above statistics are given in the *China Daily*, 4 June 1985; for commodities traded, see also *The Times*, 5 June 1986.

10. *The Times*, 13 December 1985 and *The Daily Telegraph*, 17 December 1985.

11. *The Times*, 5 February 1985.

12. Much of the foregoing is taken from an article by Chu Baotai, 'Several Theoretical and Policy Issues Concerning the Establishment of Chinese-Foreign Joint Ventures', *Guoji Maoyi Wenti* (International Trade Journal), No.5, 1983, pp. 19–22, as translated in *JPRS*, 17 February 1984; see also *The Times*, 13 December 1985.

13. *China Daily*, 6 May 1985.

14. *Xinhua News Agency* in English, 15 March 1985, as carried in *JPRS*, 17 April 1985.

15. 'FRG-PRC Joint Venture to Develop Inland-Ocean Shipping', *Duesseldorf Wirtschaftswoche*, 24 May 1985, pp.98–100, as translated in *JPRS*, 19 July 1985.

16. 'China's Dayawan Nuclear Power Plant Project', JETRO *China Newsletter*, No.57, July-August 1985, pp. 11–13.

17. *The Times*, 27 January 1986.

18. These special issues are discussed by David Dodwell's article 'Shenzhen, Special Economic Zone', *Financial Times*, 9 December 1985.

19. Hironao Kobayashi, 'Special Economic Zones and China's Open Economic Policy', JETRO *China Newsletter*, No.57, July-August 1985, pp. 14–17.

20. News of the bond issue was reported in the *China Daily*, 25 May 1986.

21. 'Dresdner Gets into Leasing Peking Style', *Financial Times*, 28 December 1984.

22. *South China Morning Post*, 22 June 1985.

23. For the Chinese viewpoint on management theory, see *Jingji Ribao*, 6 May 1985, as translated in *JPRS*, 18 June 1985; a discussion of Asian and

European techniques appears in Theodora Ting Chau, 'Leadership and Conflict Management: The East-Asian Approach', *Euro-Asia Business Review*, Vol.5, No.2, April 1986, pp. 36–41.

24. *Financial Times*, 16 January 1985; *China Daily*, 4 May 1985.

Chapter 4

1. Trade figures for the years from 1974 to 1977 appear in the *Oriental Economist* (Tokyo), March 1978; 1978 and 1981 statistics are given in the *Journal of Commerce* (New York), 31st January 1979 and 1 February 1982; EC deficits for 1979 and 1980 are discussed in the *International Herald Tribune*, 29 January 1981; the figure for 1984 appears in *The Times*, 20 July 1985; Japan's 1985 surplus was mentioned in *The Times*, 10 February 1986. For the 1986 figure, see *The Times*, 20 January 1988.

2. For the voluntary car quota, see *The Times*, 14 February 1983.

3. *Financial Times*, 24 November 1981.

4. For the duties imposed upon typewriters, see the *Financial Times*, 21 December 1984; the report on the European motor industry appears in *The Times*, 16 December 1985.

5. Austin Rover exports are mentioned in *The Times*, 24 January 1985; the Airbus deal is discussed in *ibid.*, 8 December 1986.

6. Industrial strategy in Japan is discussed at length in Chalmers Johnson, *MITI and the Japanese Miracle: The Growth of Industrial Policy, 1925–1975*, Stanford University Press, Stanford CA, 1982.

7. One such source is Misuru Wakabayashi, 'Japanese Management Career Progression', an article in the *Euro-Asia Business Review*, Vol.5, No.2, April 1986. See, especially, p. 30.

8. Much of the foregoing is drawn from *Japanese Corporate Personnel Management, Business Information Series 10*, JETRO, Tokyo, 1982.

9. Discussion of Japan's economy in general and specifics of the tax system appears in Charles Smith, 'Japan's Agenda for the Second Half of the Eighties' in *Marubeni Business Bulletin*, February 1985, pp. 5–9.

10. Details of the 1987 Japanese budget are outlined in a report from David Watts in *The Times*, 31 December 1986.

11. Details are given in an article by Derek Harris appearing in *The Times*, 30 May 1985.

12. Ibid.

13. Aspects of retailing are discussed in George Fields, 'The Impact of Changing Cultural Values on the Japanese Market', *Euro-Asia Business Review*, Vol.4, No.4, October 1985, pp. 38–42.

14. JETRO frequently publishes booklets for the benefit of foreign exporters and some of the foregoing details have been drawn from *Retailing in the Japanese Consumer Market, JETRO Marketing Series 5*, Revised 1979.

15. *The Times*, 16 January 1987.

16. *The Daily Telegraph*, 8 January 1987.

Chapter 5

1. The theme of *Nihonjinron* is pursued by Peter N. Dale, *The Myth of Japanese Uniqueness* (New York, 1985); for different, though related, arguments, see R. Mouer and Y. Sugimoto, *Images of Japanese Society* (London, 1986).

2. Relevant figures appear in *The Independent*, 13 February 1987; *The Times*, 20 January 1988; and *International Herald Tribune*, 7 July 1987.

3. *The Times*, 26 January 1988.

4. *Ibid.*, 30 January 1988.

5. *International Herald Tribune*, 16 October 1987.

6. There are many references to bodies like the 2000 group, for example, in the *Financial Times*, 4 February 1985 and *Look Japan*, 10 April 1985.

7. This figure was given in 'Japan's Manufactured Imports: 23 Case Studies', *Now in Japan*, 36, JETRO, Tokyo, 1984.

8. This issue was raised by Aurelia George in *Nakasone and the Internationalisation of Japan*, a paper presented to the Seventh New Zealand International Conference on Asian Studies, held at the University of Auckland on 15–18 May 1987.

9. References to tax reform appear in *Financial Times*, 1 February 1988; for changes in industrial structure, see 'Six trillion yen package to boost the domestic economy', *Liberal Star*, 10 August 1987.

10. Discussion of such priorities is the subject of an article by Yoshihide Ishiyama, 'Japanese Industrial Policy: Lessons for the United States', *Euro-Asia Business Review*, 6, 1, January 1987, pp. 19–24.

11. *Liberal Star*, 10 July 1987.

12. Charles Smith, 'Ups and downs of Japan-EC relations: mutual frustration lingers', *Marubeni Business Bulletin*, October 1984, pp. 6–9. Marubeni is one of Japan's major trading companies.

13. *Japan Times*, 3 June 1987.

14. *Daily Telegraph*, 30 December 1986.

15. *International Herald Tribune*, 24 June 1987.

16. For debates in the European Parliament see *The Times*, 19 January 1987; the corporate competition issue is raised by Aurelia George, *op.cit.*

17. *The Times*, 25 January 1988.

18. *Daily Telegraph*, 6 January 1986.

19. An article by R. Barry O'Brien, 'The Japanese invasion of Britain: rising sun or a false dawn' in the *Daily Telegraph*, 6 January 1986, surveys the evolution of Japanese investment and manufacturing in Britain.

20. A discussion of technological exchange and investment issues appears in Louis Turner and Michael Hodges, 'The European challenge in Japan in consumer electronics', *Euro-Asia Business Review*, 4, 1, February 1985, pp. 12–15.

21. This theme is pursued in a book review by Prabhu S. Guptara in *ibid.*, 6, 2, April 1987, pp. 46–7.

22. An article by Steve Vogel, 'Japanese expatriates in Europe: the tales of two men', *ibid.*, 5, 2, April 1986, pp. 11–18, provides some insights into these issues.

23. For these views see, for example, Teruhiko Tomita, 'Japanese Management in Britain', *ibid.*, 5, 4, October 1986, pp. 5–7. See also the report by Barrie Clement in *The Times*, 25 January 1985.

24. *The Times*, 14 January 1988.

25. *International Herald Tribune*, 22 September 1987.

26. JETRO published the summary of a lecture entitled, 'How to negotiate in Japan', given by Mr. Masao Okamoto, Managing Director of the Nomura Research Institute, on the 11th June 1980 and it is on this that much of the foregoing discussion of Japanese decision-making and negotiating style is based.

27. One writer who pursues such themes very effectively is Vladimir Pacik in 'Joint ventures with the Japanese: the key role of HRM', *Euro-Asia Business Review*, 6, 4, October 1987, pp. 36–9.

28. See a report in *The Independent*, 22 June 1987.

29. *The Times*, 7 January 1986.

30. Much of the factual information cited above has been obtained from R. Barry O'Brien, 'Japan banks poised to seize chances', *Daily Telegraph*, 7 January 1986.

31. *International Herald Tribune*, 22 June 1987.

32. *The Times*, 8 March 1988.

33. Details are given in *Daily Telegraph*, 7 January 1986.

34. Leslie S. Hiroaka, 'Financial Deregulation in Tokyo and London', *Euro-Asia Business Review*, 6, 2, April 1987, pp. 27–32.

35. *International Herald Tribune*, 22 June 1987.

36. *Financial Times*, 17 February 1986. It must nevertheless be added that, until the lifting of foreign exchange controls in 1980, foreign banks were prominent in supplying Japanese industry with foreign exchange, a sector in which Japanese banks were forbidden to take part.

37. *Sunday Express*, 31 January 1988.

38. The implications of market opening in Tokyo are discussed in a feature article in *The Times*, 11 July 1986.

39. *International Herald Tribune*, 22 June 1987.

40. 'Tokyo shrugs off the crash', *The Times*, 18 December 1987.

41. *Financial Times*, 10 March 1988.

42. *The Times*, 18 December 1987.

43. Discussion of this issue appears in *The Times*, 2 March 1987.

44. One source covering changes in employment patterns is Robert Whymant, 'High flying yen forces Japan to shed jobs', *Daily Telegraph*, 6 December 1986.

45. For an excellent analysis of these trends see Charles Smith, 'Japan's venture business boom: a new generation of industries', *Marubeni Business Bulletin*, August 1984, pp. 6–9.

46. A report from Japan by David Watts in *The Times*, 27 December 1985, discusses these issues.

47. *The Economist*, 31 October 1981.

48. Among other sources refer to 'Information and globalism', *Look Japan*, 10 March 1986, p. 9.

49. Many articles on Japan's education system have recently appeared in the media; see, for instance, *The Times Higher Education Supplement*, 12 December 1986 and 8 January 1988.

50. These shortages are discussed by Robert Whymant, 'Japan plans clampdown on unskilled immigrants', in the *Daily Telegraph*, 29 February 1988.

Chapter 6

1. F. Herbert and J. Ellison, 'Changing Sino-Soviet Relations', *Problems of Communism*, May-June 1987, pp. 27–8; see also the report in the *International Herald Tribune*, 26/27 September 1987.

2. An example of this is the article by Jiao Yuxi, 'Greater unity and strength of Western Europe contributes to world peace', in the *Chinese People's Institute of Foreign Affairs Journal*, 4, June 1987, pp. 42–7.

3. Discussion of China's initial stage of socialism appears in Zhao Ziyang, *Progressing along China's Special Social Road* (Hong Kong, 1987). This is the Chinese version of a report by Zhao Ziyang to the 13th CCP Congress held in October 1987.

4. For details, refer to Tim Luard, 'Chinese ensure no U-turn on Deng's road to reform', in the *Daily Telegraph,* 13 April 1988.

5. *International Herald Tribune,* 13 October 1987

6. This percentage was given by Carl Riskin in China's Political Economy (London, 1987).

7. A detailed analysis of these issues appears in 'Special Report: the Shanghai Economic Zone', *China Newsletter,* 71, November-December 1987, pp. 13–17.

8. For a prominent case study, see *The Times,* 5 November 1986.

9. For discussion of China's import strategy, see Ulrich Hiemenz, 'PRC prospects for trade and investment', *Euro-Asia Business Review,* 6, 3, July 1987, pp. 31–2; for China's world trade deficits see *China Newsletter,* 73, March-April 1988, p. 1; other statistics are given by *The Times,* 15 August 1987.

10. *Financial Times,* 17 December 1986.

11. For World Bank loan details see the *Daily Telegraph,* 28 March 1988.

12. Opportunities for Western investors are discussed in the *China Daily,* 14 November 1985; development strategy is included in a report on the National People's Congress in the *Daily Telegraph,* 14 April 1988.

13. *The Times,* 28 March 1988; investment percentages for particular countries during the period from 1979 to 1985 appear in Ulrich Hiemenz, 'PRC prospects for trade and investment', *Euro-Asia Business Review,* 6, 3, July 1987, p. 33.

14. *The Times,* 5 February 1988; for Total's venture see the *Financial Times,* 18 December 1986.

15. This agreement was reported in *The Times,* 25 February 1988.

16. Such experiments are discussed in John Thoburn, 'China's Special Economic Zones revisited', *Euro-Asia Business Review,* 5, 4, October 1986, pp. 44–9.

17. There are many sources dealing with the introduction of management education to China and its attendant problems. The following are examples: Max Boisot, 'Management training in the People's Republic of China: the task ahead', *Euro-Asia Business Review,* 6, 2, April 1987, pp. 12–14; J. M. Livingstone, 'Chinese Management in Flux', *Euro-Asia Business Review,* 6, 2, April 1987, pp. 15–20; see also Dorothy J. Solinger, *Chinese Business under Socialism: the Politics of Domestic Commerce,* 1949–1980 (Berkeley, California, 1984).

18. Details appear in *The Times,* 28 August 1987 and the *Daily Telegraph* 7 April 1988.

19. Much comment on Japanese defence policy appeared in the Western press during 1987 and 1988. See, for example, a report by Robert Whymant, 'Soviet military build-up poses threat to Japan', the *Daily Telegraph,* 28 August 1987, and Lisa Martineau, 'Japan is urged to arm island', *The Guardian,* 1 March 1988.

20. This theme is pursued in an article by Geoffrey Smith in *The Times,* 26 April 1988.

21. Note, in this context, the editorial on Mr. Takeshita's visit in *The Times,* 5 May 1988.

22. *Ibid.,* 12 April 1988.

23. *Financial Times,* 11 March 1988.

24. *The Times,* 26 April 1988.

25. See the report in *The Times,* 14 April 1988.

26. R. Drifte, *Arms Production in Japan* (Boulder, Colorado, 1986).

27. Japan's arms technology is discussed at some length in R. Drifte, *Arms Production in Japan* (Boulder, Colorado, 1986). Speculation about arms purchases from Britain appears in a report in *The Times,* 2 January 1988.

28. Details appear in the *Daily Telegraph,* 17 March 1988.

29. *The Times,* 25 February 1988.

30. For an account of trends in Japanese share prices see the *Daily Telegraph,* 7 April 1988.

Select Bibliography

Bachman, D. M., *Chen Yun and the Chinese Political System* (University of California, 1985).

Baerwald, H. H., *Party Politics in Japan* (Allen and Unwin, 1986).

Barnett, A. D., *China's Economy in Global Perspective* (Brookings Institution, 1981).

Chi, W. S., *Ideological Conflicts in Modern China: democracy and authoritarianism* (Transaction Books, 1986).

Chossudovsky, M., *Towards Capitalist Restoration?: Chinese Socialism after Mao* (St. Martin's Press, 1986).

Dale, P. N., *The Myth of Japanese Uniqueness* (Croom Helm, 1986).

Drifte, R., *Arms Production in Japan* (Westview Press, 1986).

JETRO, *Japanese Corporate Personnel Management* (Business Information Series 10, 1982).

JETRO, *Retailing in the Japanese Consumer Market* (Marketing Series 5, revised, 1985).

Johnson, C., *MITI and the Japanese Miracle: the Growth of Industrial Policy, 1925–1975* (Stanford University Press, 1982).

Kamata, S., *Japan in the Passing Lane: an Insider's Account of life in a Japanese Auto factory* (Pantheon Books, 1982).

Kobayashi, T., *Society, Schools and Progress in Japan* (Pergamon Press, 1976).

Kueh, Y. Y., *Economic Planning and Local Mobilization in post-Mao China* (Contemporary China Institute, School of Oriental and African Studies, University of London, 1985).

Laaksonen, O., *Management in China* (de Gruyter, 1988).

Lee, P. N. S., *Industrial Management and Economic Reform in China, 1949-1984* (OUP, 1987).

McMillan, C. J., *The Japanese Industrial System* (de Gruyter, 1989).

Macpherson, W. J., *The Economic Development of Japan* (Macmillan, 1987).

Mouer, R. and Y. Sugimoto, *Images of Japanese Society* (KPI, 1986).

Oborne, M. *China's Special Zones* (OECD, 1986).

Perkins, D. H., *China's Modern Economy in Historical Perspective* (Stanford University Press, 1975).

Perkins, D. H., *China: Asia's Next Economic Giant* (University of Washington Press, 1986).

Riskin, C., *China's Political Economy* (OUP, 1987).

Solinger, D. J., *Chinese Business under Socialism: the Politics of Domestic Commerce, 1949–1980* (University of California Press, 1984).

Scalapino, R. A., *The Foreign Policy of Modern Japan* (University of California Press, 1977).

Taylor, R., *China's Intellectual Dilemma* (University of British Columbia Press, 1981).

Thomas, R. M. and T. N. Postlethwaite, *Schooling in East Asia* (Pergamon Press, 1983).

Wilkinson, E., *Japan versus Europe* (Penguin Books, 1983).

Wong, K. Y. and K. Y. Chu, *Modernisation in China: the Case of the Shenzhen Special Economic Zone* (OUP, 1985).

Index